Francis Charles Sessios

From the Land of the Midnight Sun to the Volga

Francis Charles Sessios

From the Land of the Midnight Sun to the Volga

ISBN/EAN: 9783744743570

Printed in Europe, USA, Canada, Australia, Japan

Cover: Foto ©Andreas Hilbeck / pixelio.de

More available books at **www.hansebooks.com**

From the

Land of the Midnight Sun

To the Volga.

FROM THE

Land of the Midnight Sun

TO THE

Volga

BY FRANCIS C. SESSIONS

President of the Ohio Historical and Archæological Society

Illustrated by E. W. DEMING

New York
WELCH, FRACKER COMPANY
1890

COPYRIGHT 1890, BY WELCH, FRACKER CO.

From the Land of the Midnight Sun to the Volga.

I.

TRAVELING TOWARD THE MIDNIGHT SUN.

WE left Copenhagen with regret; it was one of the most attractive cities we had seen. Prince Bonaparte, of France, arrived at our hotel, just before we left, with his wife and five servants. He had the peculiar Bonaparte nose and features, and it was at least interesting to look at the descendant of one who became so prominent in the world's history.

We crossed by steamer the Malmo Sound to Malmo, and here first entered Sweden, and took cars for Gottenborg. The country through which we pass looks much like the northern part of Vermont and New

Hampshire, with its stony fields and stonewall fences, red houses and barns, white birch trees, brooks, small lakes full of water lilies, white meeting houses, and the old-fashioned well-sweep for drawing water, which we used to see in boyhood days fifty years ago.

Our first dinner in Sweden was peculiar in finding a table loaded with food, and everyone pitching in for themselves. There are no servants, and if you do not get enough to eat, it is your own fault. The good-heartedness of the Scandinavians is proverbial, and it was first observed on giving a little girl ten ore, equal to one cent—she shook hands with all of us, and curtsied several times.

We begin at once to see why Sweden is called the Land of Three Thousand Lakes, for we pass lakes continually. We stop over night at Gottenborg. We were fortunate again in having a letter to another son of Professor Sinding, who is connected with the largest cable and telegraph construction company in Europe. He went with us over the city, and we noticed canals and bridges in every direction, reminding us of Amsterdam.

Gottenborg is a beautiful city, and in our

ride to the Oreas Mountain, to get a view of the city and surrounding country, we passed numerous pleasant-looking villas. One at the foot of the Oreas is owned by Oscar Dickson, the wealthiest man in Scandinavia, who has fitted out several scientific expeditions to the Arctic Ocean. Professor Nordenskjold is at the head of the last expedition, and on account of his scientific attainments was offered by King Oscar the title of Baronet, which he refused.

At this place the celebrated Gottenborg licensing system was first adopted. We have heard it discussed in the United States a great deal, and I was anxious to know how it worked, as many opinions have been expressed in regard to its effect in restraining drinking. Our friend, Mr. Sinding, spoke highly of the good results, and said that drunkenness had diminished greatly. The leading feature of the system of licensing, or rather of non-licensing, is that a temperance company is formed to buy licenses and existing rights, and to open a limited number of shops for the sale of pure and unadulterated spirits, and control the sale to proper persons, and none in small quantities to drunkards, the manager having no interest in the sale of the spirits. After deducting interest at the rate of five per cent. on the capital expended, the company hands the whole of the surplus profits over to the municipality. Mr. Sinding said the profit was large, and was used for helping the poor, etc., of the city. I have learned its good effects in many of the cities in Sweden and Norway, and I shall try to get all the information I can in regard to it. All the larger cities in Scandinavia are adopting it.

Our train to Christiana followed, for some distance, the Trollhatta Canal, which is one of the most remarkable products of engineering skill, uniting Gottenborg and Stockholm, and uniting the Vennor and Veltor Lakes with the Gota River. The greatest difficulty met with was the Trollhatta Falls, which are a succession of rapids about one hundred and twenty feet high, one of the finest falls in Sweden, but to us who have Niagara and Yosemite Falls, did not seem worth hardly a notice.

The great Swedenborg, who was a native of Stockholm, I believe, was one of the engineers to draw plans for the erection of sluices at Trollhatta, commissioned by King Karl XII., at the beginning of the eighteenth century. The whole length of the canal is two hundred and forty miles. It is quite a curiosity to see the large steamers going through the locks as if going up a steep precipice. We noticed printed on our cars as follows : "*Gjennemgaaende till Christiana*," which means through to Christiana.

On passing the line from Sweden to Norway we notice at once a different country, for it is the mountains which separate Sweden from Norway. From the flat country of the former we have the mountains and picturesque views of the latter. The houses are painted yellow. All the stations are beautiful architectural depots. The farmers are cutting their grass, and the curious poles, about eight feet high, stuck up around the meadows, we could not understand, until we saw them placing the cut grass around them to dry. In some fields long poles are put horizontally, and the hay is laid upon them to dry, the season being so wet and uncertain, that it is necessary for them to hang up the grass so that the wind may help the sun in drying it.

Christiana, the capital of Norway, is reached, and although nine o'clock at night, the sun is just setting. Our dinner is announced, and we find a great variety of cold meats and cold fish. We have been traveling all day and are hungry, and after we have fully satisfied our appetites, we are told that the hot meats are now ready. Only a few could remain to digest the hot meats. Afterward we were told that it is customary in Norway to have the cold meats first.

We leave Christiana by the steamer Orion, and we enjoy the delightful scenery down the Christiana Fjord for seventy miles, until we come to the stormy Skagarrak. It is about two thousand six hundred miles to the North Cape and return. The fjords are numerous. One, the Trondjhem, is one hundred and twenty miles long. A fjord is an arm of the sea and is pronounced ford. The scenery the first day is picturesque and grand, with Christiana in the background, and numerous islands and hills covered with yellow houses, looking in the distance like children's play-houses, and the little steamers and sail-boats plying hither and thither. We soon come to Horten, an important naval station, where the fjord is five miles wide. In some places, however, it is only five hundred feet wide. It is a splendid situation for a fort, and well sheltered.

A short distance from here, at Gokstad Sandefjord, is the mound which contained the "Viking Galley," which is now in Christiana. We soon leave behind us the rich, green vegetation, and nothing is seen but the barren rocks, which almost touch each other from island to island. As we go out to sea it begins to grow stormy and rough, and the old stórmy Skagarrak keeps up its reputation. Most of the passengers had left the deck for their berths, only two of us remained "to fight it out on that line," if it took all night. Soon my companion succumbed, and rushed to the side of the ship and showed signs of distress. I was determined to keep my reputation as a good sailor, gained by crossing the Atlantic five times, and the English channel, and the Irish and North seas a number of times without being sick, but at last old "Skagarrak" conquered.

We were glad to leave the ship at Ekersund, two hundred miles from Christiana, and charter a train on a little railroad running across the promontory twenty-eight miles, and escape a rougher sea, and wait the arrival of the steamer at Staranger. This little road is built on purpose to accommodate passengers on the steamers, who want to escape the most stormy place to the North Cape. Although the road is only twenty-eight miles long, it is so crooked that it took our express two and one-half hours to run the distance.

We are glad to get to this quaint old city of Bergen, with its thirty thousand to forty thousand population, and after getting well domiciled at our hotel, make for the Bergen bank to draw some money. The main street is called "Strandgarden." We are at once amused at the Norwegian dress of the women, so odd and quaint, with their high, white caps, and large white capes, and new and yellow bands, and bright handkerchiefs and bodices, and heavy, plain woolen dresses, with full, plain skirts and wooden shoes. We get the wrong direction to the bank and step into a dry goods store, and make out to ask them the way to the bank, and they send with us a clerk to show the way. On arriving we find a splendid banking room. We were struck at the absence of protection from thieves around the teller's counter, and, looking around, find that I am the only one of the customers with my hat on. When they come into the bank they take off their hats and seat themselves on a bench, until their turn comes to be waited upon; no talking, except on their business, and then only in a low tone.

When my business was finished I looked around and found the same young clerk who had come in with me to show me back to my hotel; I tried to make him understand that I was obliged to him, but that I was going to the fish market, this being Saturday, and the greatest fish market in the world; he finally shook hands and left me—everywhere the people are so kind and attentive.

The fish market is curious enough; the end of the harbor comes up to the side of Torvet Square, and along the quay are three horizontal iron railings, and on the water side the numerous fishing boats come up, bows inward, the fish lying loose all over the boat, and the owners stand and barter with the customers on the quay, and hand down their buckets to get the fish. I did not see as beautiful a display of fish even at the great Fishery Exhibition at London, which had just been opened at Hyde Park, when we were there.

Here were all sizes and colors, some large ones resembling in color our gold fish, some with all the colors of the rainbow; large, splendid salmon; another like our white fish, but much larger. We have seen only one meat shop in Bergen; fish is cheap and plentiful, and seems to be the main article of food. All along the wharf were vessels unloading their dried codfish, which were piled up like cordwood, filling the warehouses; these fish, we understood, are shipped to Spain and other Catholic countries, where they do not eat meat on Fridays.

On our walk about the city we see some terrible scurvy-disease covering the faces, ears, hands, arms and bodies of some of the people. We learn that it is leprosy. This frightful disease is prevalent in Norway among the peasants, especially on the coast, on account of eating so much salt-fish without vegetables, and also due to a lack of nourishing food, and living in damp houses, where they salt the fish. We passed a hospital for lepers, and the lepers are not allowed to marry, so that a hereditary disease is kept in check.

In front of a great fur store we see skins of fresh-killed bears, and those of other wild animals; a large trade is done here in furs. The Gottenborg temperance plan is in vogue here, and we have seen only two drunken persons, one was a colored sailor from Africa, and he was more of curiosity than a monkey show the other side of the street, on account of his color.

Our Sunday in old Bergen was a most delightful one; the weather was cool and the sun shown bright, which is an unusual thing, and it has the reputation of being the most uncertain place as to weather in Europe; a pleasant day is an exception; the people were out *en masse*, and the churches were crowded, judging from the three Lutheran churches which we attended, and many of the worshippers had to stand up.

We could not understand a word the priest (the ministers are all called priests in Scandinavia) said, but he had an earnest, scholarly manner, and held the attention of the audience closely to the end; he wore a gown and had on a high, wide ruffle, which made him look like the old pictures of John Huss or Calvin. The ritual was simple; almost the whole service was sung, even the scripture was monotoned. The precentor, in a black frock coat, stood on one side of the priest and faced toward him instead of the choir and congregation; the singing was slow and drawling.

I learn that there are scarcely any churches in Norway or Sweden, but the state churches, which are orthodox Lutheran, and religion seems to have a strong hold upon the people. The priests are state officials, and are paid to perform prescribed duties by the state, and they must be graduates of a university.

After the communion service there was a large number of babies presented for baptism. The priest, after reading the ritual, went around and made the sign of the cross with his hands over the face of each babe, and then he went around and blessed each one ; then the mothers came forward to the front, and he read the covenant to them, and took water in his hands and poured it over the head of the child three times, and said, "Father, Son, and Holy Ghost."

We noticed, as we visited the cemetery, to see the grave of Ole Bull, who was a native of Bergen, and was buried here, that there was a large number of women and girls washing off the monuments and gravestones, and placing beautiful bouquets of flowers upon the graves. We understand this is the pleasant custom every Saturday night through the summer, and in the winter evergreens are used. Roses and flowers had

ICELANDERS.

just made their appearance this summer, and this was the first Sunday for flower decorating this year; and more than usual attention was given to mowing the grass and making everything attractive for the masses who visit the hallowed spot on Sunday. Ole Bull's grave was in the center of the cemetery, where walks extend from east to west and north to south. There was no stone to mark his grave, but the earth was raised over it, and it was covered with English ivy, and on the top was a beautiful bouquet and a number of white pond lilies.

We had a beautiful sun, although at nine o'clock at night, and I never saw the sky, even in Italy, more soft and mellow.

On our way to the hotel we noticed the servant girls were scouring the brass knobs of the doors and washing the entrances. This is also the custom every Saturday night.

We never saw such beautiful calceolarias and pelargoniums as are at the windows of almost every house. As we passed up the most beautiful street for private residences, there were many villas high up on the mountain side, overlooking the two lakes and the fjord. The street is called "King Oscar's Garden," and the flags were flying from the residences of the different consuls residing on the street; and from a beautiful villa we noticed the stars and stripes, which looked to us more beautiful than ever in comparison with the others; and then it reminded us, in this far off land, of our home, and we took off our hats in reverence of the old flag.

The little dun-colored Norwegian horses, more like ponies, are very tough and intelligent, and when you go past them, one feels like patting them, they look at one so responsively. When the driver stops them in the street, and wishes to leave them, he fastens a cord to the cariole and then around the horse's foot, just below the fetlock. We had quite an experience in ordering a cariole for an evening ride. We wanted one with one horse and places for two persons, instead of that we found at the door of the hotel one cariole with two horses and seats for four persons, and one cariole with one horse and for one person. The liveryman thought we ought to take them as they were ordered the day before, and were in great demand. We had the pleasure, therefore, of inviting our party to take an evening ride with us; so much for not speaking the language.

The ride, by steamer, among the thousands of islands, with the bare rocks and curious shapes, some as high as three thousand feet, and the water falls, are almost as grand as the Yosemite valley, in California, and as picturesque as Lake George, in our own country, and Lake Lucerne in Switzerland; and all this scenery continues along the coast of one thousand miles. We stop at several fishing towns, and get off the steamer to take a look at the natives. The women all look sad and bent over, with their eyes cast on the ground, high cheek-bones and low foreheads, and wear coarse flannel dresses and high-colored shawls upon their heads.

Some of the towns are situated on three or four islands, and little steamers go and come, which give them the appearance of a miniature Venice. We are glad to come to Throndhjem, and remain three or four days, and take excursions into the country, and can well unite with the old song, "Det er saa in ferest in Throndhjem hvile," "'Tis so pleasant in Throndhjem to dwell." It is about the latitude of southern Iceland, and the largest northermost town in Europe, and has a population of from twenty to twenty-five thousand.

Throndhjem was the old capital of Norway until the liberation in 1814; it lies on a peninsula, and on the beautiful fjord, after which it is named, and which we had just come up. The cathedral here is the oldest and finest in Scandinavia, and is built on the spot where Saint Olaf was buried, and attracts to this place multiudes of pilgrims from Norway and other countries. Olaf landed here in A. D. 995, he found the people pagans; having himself been converted through English missionaries, he came to Norway from that land and set about converting the people, and to him is given the credit of converting the Norwegians to the Christian religion.

Olaf was killed in a great battle fought near here in 1030, and he has been ever since regarded as the patron saint of the Scandinavian churches; and Christianity became permanently and securely fixed in spite of the political and religious disturbances. The great cathedral erected to his memory, and having been several times nearly destroyed, is being restored. In the eleventh and twelfth centuries the kings of Norway were buried here; by the Constitution of Norway all the sovereigns of the country are required to come to Throndhjem to be crowned in the cathedral. Oscar II., the present King, and the Queen came here in 1873, and the ceremony was performed in this old cathedral; thus the memory of Saint Olaf is kept fresh in the minds of the people. Our courier informed us that Longfellow spent some time in Norway, and translated a poem, which, if I remember correctly, was entitled, "Saint Olaf." The first line of one verse is

"Saint Olaf, he rideth over the plain."

The views from the mountain called Bloesevoldbakken, which we ascended, rewarded us well for the tiresome walk, as did also a walk to a beautiful waterfall, called Lerfos, upper and lower.

The United States Consul informs us that the exportations from the United States are increasing, and consist mostly of petroleum and agricultural machines, and other articles are finding their way here; I noticed our steamer unloading at one of the docks kegs of paint marked "Gloucester, Mass."

The words of the Norwegian language seem so long that it is almost impossible to pronounce them, and some seem odd enough to us; over a book store was a sign with, "Bog-og Papierhandle," on it, which means Book and Paper Store.

The living at the hotels is abundant; we have several kinds of fish at every meal and various kinds of meat, including bear and reindeer flesh. The air is cool and bracing, and one feels ready to do full justice at every meal.

After passing through an infinity of small islands, we come to an island called Torgen, with a mountain called Torghatta (marked hat). The mountain, eight hundred feet high, resembles a hat; our steamer stops, that all who desire may ascend and observe an aperture through the mountain; it is about sixty-two feet high, and one can see through the aperture the distant sea with the vessels and shipping.

II.

THE TORGHATTA MOUNTAINS. LAPLAND. HAMMERFEST. CHARACTER OF THE LAPS.

THERE is a legend connected with Torghatta Mountain which represents "a giantess who was pursued by her lover while her brother attempted to rescue her. The torghatta, or hat, of the latter, having been pierced by an arrow shot by the amorous lover, the sun shone through the aperture, and metamorphosed the distressed maiden into stone—the pursuer being, at this juncture, only one hundred and five miles away!" In passing the giantess the natives sometimes raise their hats with mock ceremony.

At one place a bride and groom came aboard, and a large number of boats with young people accompanied them to the steamer. It was a gay scene, as the steamer departed, to see the girls flirt their handkerchiefs with the words "Farvell! farvell!" The word is spelled with a *v;* there is no *w* in the Norwegian language, and *v* is used instead.

At Svolvaer, a fishing town, we go ashore, and find only a few houses on the rocks, and all over the town are posters announcing a theatre. We inquire for the theatre, and are pointed to a tent; the performance is unique enough, and is easily moved from place to place for the amusement of the poor fishermen and their families.

All these towns are occupied by the families of fishermen who are off to the Lofodon Islands and other places. We have on board two officials of the Norwegian Government, who are intelligent, and give us much valuable information. In speaking of these fishermen, one of the officials said, at one of the islands he called on the priest, where there was a small church, and inquiring in regard to his success, the priest replied: "Our church and our cemetery are occupied by women and children. You go into the latter, and you will only see the graves of women and children; all the men are drowned at the fisheries; sometimes as large a number as five hundred will be lost at one time in a terrible storm."

We soon arrive in Lapland, and a number

A LAPLAND HUT.

of Laps come on board, and are a great curiosity to us all. They say that they have only a small herd of reindeer, and have just come over from Sweden. Their dress is of reindeer skins, and is very peculiar, quite as odd as the dress of Indians. There are about twenty thousand Laplanders in Norway, and in all Scandinavia only thirty thousand. It seems as if they are dwindling away as fast as the Indians of North America. The Laps once dominated the whole of Scandinavia. They were once a race of hunters, and the reindeer is the whole source of their wealth, and was, no doubt, formerly an object of chase only.

We arrive at Tromsoe, the capital of Lapland, and take a walk through the old town, but defer our visit to their camp and herds of reindeer until our return from the land of the midnight sun.

We have been remaining up all night to witness the sun, that does not go below the horizon in this region for nearly three months—from May to August—and does not appear for nearly three months in the winter; it is dark from December first until the last of January, so that lamps have to be used all the time. When light comes, they celebrate it with firing of guns, dancing and a general holiday. There has been no darkness since we entered the Arctic circle; indeed, for several days we could see to read all night. At Tromsoe we sat up all night to watch the sun, and, as it does not set, we expected to see it; but the mountains intervened, and we did not see it at twelve midnight, but could see its rays on all the distant mountains in the west, and on the hill sides. It had a peculiar rosy hue, and was one of the most attractive views in our life. We did not get a view of the sun itself until about one o'clock in the morning.

We arrive at Hammerfest, the most northern town in Europe, or, I believe, in the world, and leave at once for the North Cape, and remain up all night, and at twelve midnight the Captain sounds the whistle, and the sun is about twice the size of its disc above the horizon, a shout goes up, and we have a splendid view of the midnight sun, and are well satisfied with our journey of nearly five thousand miles to see it.

The sun at twelve midnight was one half a point east of north; it seemed to move along the horizon for awhile and then commenced rising in the heavens. We steam along with intense interest for North Cape, watching the sun all the time. We cannot express our feelings, all is hushed in silence. Carlyle revels in the idea that " while all nations are asleep, we stand here in the presence of that great power which will wake them all."

Each one has his own peculiar thoughts, and much has been written, but words fail to express our individual sensation. We have read and studied in our geography, half a century ago, that in this part of the world the sun shone all the time for six months, and darkness reigned for six months, but it is a little less than three months.

We soon reach the North Cape, and go ashore in our little boats to ascend the cape, which is about one thousand feet high. The ascent is steep and rugged. Creeping, sometimes on our hands and knees, with singular feelings about the region we are in, we get to the top and walk about three miles to the end of the promontory over the rocky ascent, until we look off toward that great unknown Arctic ocean, and it seems as if we had come to the end of the earth, and were gazing upon the confines of the eternal regions, that we saw in the distance the outlines of the land of which it is said "there is no night there."

We are told that we are only two days' sail from the original ice, and that three days' sail will take us as far north as where the Jeanette was lost. On the top was a monument, erected to the memory of the time, in July, eighteen hundred and seventy-three, when King Oscar II. visited the place. It was a granite shaft seven feet high, imbedded in a strong stone wall. Last winter it was blown over, showing the great power of the wind here.

We take a last look at the ocean, and a Russian steamer is in view, which is supposed to be hunting for whales. A few other fishing boats are seen. On our way down we gather some twenty varieties of arctic flowers, some very beautiful, and the ladies take them to press as a memento of this visit.

When we arrive at the ship the fishing lines are out, and those that remained had their own sport fishing for flounders. We have had flounders for breakfast, flounders for dinner, and flounders for supper; and we expect, when we get on the sea, from all accounts of the roughness of the voyage around the cape, we shall get *floundered* all night, or, rather, I forgot there is no night here. We have got about used to sleeping during the time that it is day here, and watching the sun when it is night with us in America.

We stop at the *Norpolanhotel* (North Pole Hotel), and the fishy smell all over the old town of Hammerfest is terrible to endure. About fifty fishing vessels are starting off for the fisheries, and it is an interesting sight. Such jabbering and talking is jargon itself. On the high rocks on shore are the women and children of the fishermen, watching their fathers and brothers, who may never return, depart.

There are large herds of reindeer near here, and the laps are about the town, selling their reindeer shoes, and other things peculiar to their habits.

This town of Hammerfest was a scene of British arrogance in 1853. It seems that some English merchants here wanted to get some of their goods into port for less than the duty, and the authorities confiscated them. After considerable talk in Parliament, two men-of-war were sent here, and demanded of the authorities sixty thousand pounds sterling, or two hundred and forty thousand dollars, else they would bombard the town. Finally, the Norze bank, in Christiana, agreed to advance the money and save the town, and they were to pay so much per year. It was a great sacrifice for so poor a town.

We leave this wonderful region with regret; it would be delightful to stay and see the sun in its present condition for weeks, and visit the fishing places in the vicinity. Fishing is the entire income, and when the fish fail the people are poor enough; last year was a bad season and the whole business of Norway is affected by it. From all accounts the fishermen of Spitzbergen have struck a "bonanza." Report has just come that five fishermen from Hammerfest had shot five hundred seals in eighteen hours, and could have taken more, but their guns became too hot. The men lie flat on the ice and when the seals' heads appear above the water shoot them.

I take another look at the North Cape and call to mind the words of our own Longfellow:

> "And there uprose before me
> Upon the water's edge,
> The huge and haggard shape
> Of that unknown North Cape,
> Whose form is like a wedge."—

which seems to stand like a rocky battlement

against the dashing water from the North Pole.

Our visit to the camp of the Laplanders from Tromsoe was exceedingly interesting; we walked over a rough country for some distance, and in a valley under the mountains came suddenly upon their huts; they are made of sticks stuck in the ground, dome-shaped, and covered with sod, with a hole in the top to let out the smoke from the fire in the center over which a pot is suspended.

We peeped in and all looked so forbidding that we hesitated to go in, for fear of fleas and dirt. Around the wigwam or hut sat several women at work making shoes of reindeer hides, spoons of their horns, purses and various articles to sell. The dogs were having a fight and things did not look inviting, but I ventured in and was glad enough to retreat at once.

A short distance from the encampment was a herd of reindeer numbering four or five hundred, and another drove was coming down the mountains; they were a great curiosity to us, with their long horns, and looked much like our deer, only larger; they are mainly used for their milk, and are milked twice a week, and their milk is the chief food of the Laps. We tasted some of it and found it too strong to drink without diluting with water. We did not get a sledge ride after reindeer, on account of the snow being wanting, but we saw some of their sledges which are made in the shape of a small boat or skiff. The reindeer are attached to the sledge and the Lap drives with a rope, and from all accounts the ride must be an exhilerating one.

The Laps in this encampment own about five or six thousand reindeer, they are worth about four dollars each and are scattered about the mountains in different herds; when they are allowed to go out of the pen they present an interesting sight, as they wind their way up the mountain, with the dogs keeping them from running away, and the unearthly screeches of the Laps add zest to the scene.

The Laplanders are of Mongolian type, small of statue, high cheek bones, low forehead, light hair, small boned and little muscles. The dress of the men and women is the same, and it is difficult to distinguish them apart—the only way to do so was from the longer tangled hair of the women.

We were quite interested in a little blue-eyed baby, strapped into a kind of birch-

LAPLANDERS' CAMP.

bark cradle or shell, with a hole at one end; the shape was like an elongated egg, and the mother had a strap across her back and held it in that way while about her work or when going from camp to camp.

The girls have a primitive way of weaving fancy-colored garters to sell; they attach a cord to a white birch bush, and drop down upon the ground, with the different colored threads in their hands, the work is all done with the hands, no shuttle, and the ladies thought it quite ingenious.

Their dress is of reindeer skins, trimmed with bright red flannel, with a long frock reaching to their knees, with a belt around the waist, in which they carry a knife; they wear a round cap made of reindeer skins, which is also trimmed with red flannel.

They are a dirty, filthy-looking people, and look as if they never used ablutions. They seemed as much interested in the dress of the ladies of our party as we were in theirs, and they would walk around the ladies, pointing to each other at what seemed to amuse them, and asking for pins.

We understand from a missionary, who was on our steamer, that the Government of Norway sends teachers and preachers among them, and they are doing all they can to elevate them; they have their children all confirmed by the Lutheran missionaries, but as they are continually wandering about from place to place, it is difficult to make much impression in civilizing them. They are allowed to intermarry with the Swedes and Norwegians, and in time may become entirely extinct as a race; a great change from the powerful race which once dominated the whole of Scandinavia. They are an honest people, and farmers say they never intrude.

In Sweden and Finland the Laps are usually divided into fisher, mountain and forest Laps; the latter two are the true representatives of the race. In Norway they are classed as sea Laps, river Laps and mountain Laps; the first two settled, the last wandering or nomadic. Their habits are most conservative, and can hardly have altered since the far distant time when they first tamed the reindeer. Reindeer form the chief wealth of the Laps, and Thompson's lines may still be taken as an accurate description of the uses to which their skins and horns are put, although one would think spoons more likely than cups to be carved out of the latter; but then where would a great deal of poetry be.

if the poet could not draw on his poetic license at pleasure; perhaps, however, Thomson alluded to the milk—

" The reindeer form their riches ; these their tents,
  Their robes, their beds, and all their homely wealth
  Supply ; their wholesome food and cheerful cups."

The mountain Laps have learned to drink coffee and wear stout Norwegian cloth, but they set as much store by the reindeer as ever. A poor family will have fifty and upward in a herd, the middle classes three hundred to seven hundred, and the richest one thousand or more. The reindeer is as beloved by the Lap as his pig by the Irishman, and the reindeer often sleep in his hut in much the same fashion. The Lap will whisper to his reindeer when harnessing him to his sleigh, and will tell him where he is to go, and declares he understands him. The reindeer is much like a stag, only smaller ; all the people, animals and trees in Lapland are very diminutive, the men are mostly under five feet high, and the women under four feet nine inches ; so great are the rigors of the climate in this, as in all countries under the Arctic circle, the cows, sheep and goats are all small in proportion. In summer the reindeer feed upon grass, and give excellent milk ; in winter they feed upon moss, which they scratch up under great depths of snow with marvellous instinct.

III.

THE REINDEER. DRESS AND HABITS OF THE NATIVES. PEASANT LIFE IN THE VALLEYS.

WHEN winter draws near great numbers of reindeer are killed and the flesh is dried and smoked to provide when the ground is covered with snow, and but few birds, like ptarmigan, partridges and caper-cailzie, are met with; the flesh is very nutritious, and after a course of grass-feeding it is surprising how soon the reindeer become fat and plump. The skin makes their dresses and boots, the sinews their thread and fishing-lines, and the horns their spoons and domestic utensils; their utensils are not all horn; the Laps have always some kettles of copper and iron, and sometimes also bowls of wood and tin; and among the rich they are even of silver.

The wandering Laps usually live in rude huts, formed of trees or poles, in the shape of a cone, with an opening in the center to allow the smoke to escape, and a few mats are spread on the floor. Each side of the fire-place is divided into three chambers, separated by mats or skins, the innermost for husband and wife, the next for the children, and the outer for servants. When the family is too poor to have servants they often find room for some reindeer.

The winter dwellings are much more substantial, and are roofed with beams, on which are hung the dried cakes of reindeer flesh, while, outside, the huts are covered with bushes and earth. The door is very low and small, and can only be entered by crawling on the hands and knees. The windows are made from the intestines of seals, prepared and sewed together. The furniture is very primitive. Such as it is, it is made by the men, who also do the cooking, and make the boats and sleighs, *skiddor*, or snow shoes, and the bows and arrows. Sometimes these winter-huts are made large enough to contain a dozen families, the separation being effected by curtains of skins.

The Lap, as he appears in his own country, is very different from many of the pictures so familiar to us. His usual dress consists of dirty old reindeer pelts and a filthy peaked cap. In winter, all the dress is made of reindeer skins, except the cap, which is made of cloth, and shaped like a sugar-loaf.

The dress of the men and women is much alike. They wear their hair long and straight, falling down the sides of the head and back; and as beards and whiskers are never seen, it is usual to distinguish between men and women by the boots. The men wear long and the women short ones. The costume is in the "Bloomer" style, and consists of a short coat of skin made with the hair outside. This is fastened around the waist with a belt and buckle, and a pair of tight-fitting breeches, made of tanned reindeer leather, are fastened round the ankle. The boots, of corresponding material, are peaked and turned up at the toes. These are drawn over the breeches and fastened at the top with a long piece of list, which keeps out the snow and makes them nearly water-tight.

Even in the depths of winter the Laps have their necks always bare. They wear no linen or stockings, and stuff the boots, which are very roomy, with soft hay, made from the cypress-grass. Their gloves are like mittens, and often ornamented with great taste. In summer, the same leather breeches are worn, but the coat is made of coarse cloth. The women carry a tobacco pouch, pipe, scissors, and a spoon to drink spirits from, hanging from the waist. The richer Laps often ornament these articles with silver braid.

In the winter the Laps use snow-shoes, or *skiddor*, and they always carry a spear, with a four-edged spike, about a foot in length, mounted on an aspen shaft, six feet long. Their equipment for the winter is completed with an old skin knap-sack for provisions, a rough case-knife in the belt, and a little iron pipe for their delectation in smoking, and sometimes a gun like a pea-rifle.

The sleighs are like small boats cut in half, and only hold one person, and are so cranky that the driver is obliged to use a short pole to keep the sleigh steady; so that between driving the reindeer, which are fastened to the sleigh, and keeping his balance with the short pole, he has enough to do. If the sleigh turns over, which it sometimes does, the occupant can not fall out, as he is too tightly packed in with skins; but he has an awkward time of it, and gets sadly bumped in the snow if the reindeer dash off at full speed, as they have a habit of doing.

The Laps all live by fishing and hunting. Their game is elk, bear, foxes, wolves, ermine and squirrel. The Russian Laps are chiefly fishers. They are quiet, hospitable, honest and inoffensive, and decidedly favorable specimens of a semi-civilized race, still retaining their patriarchal traditions. The father is supreme in the family, and can apportion his property at death, and disinherit any of his children, should he see fit. If a son wishes to leave the house and set up for himself, he can take nothing with him but his wife's dowry. Drunkenness is their great failing.

Our ride on the steamer (Damskibe) "Orion" has been three weeks. We have had an opportunity to see the whole coast of Norway, with its hundreds of fjords and lakes and an infinity of islands, and its numerous towns and cities, all supported by its immense fisheries. At one place, which we passed on our return, they told us that they had that day a great success in a "catch" of two hundred thousand herring. What we saw were being packed, on a number of islands, by men, women and children, and our steamer was taking them away from every town to Bergen, whence they are shipped to Spain and other countries. At every stopping place the steamer does not go up to the wharf, but anchors some distance off, and the numerous boats come out to bring passengers and take others ashore. Sometimes as many as twenty or thirty boats push around the steamer to get the first opportunity to discharge their loads. Oftentimes quite a skirmish ensues between them.

While this is going on, other boat loads of men and women are in the distance, waving their handkerchiefs to friends leaving on the steamers, making an exciting scene, and is an oasis to the passengers who have such long distances to travel, with nothing to relieve the monotony, save the splendid scenery, with a surprise at every turn.

A London gentleman and myself concluded that we would leave the steamer at Throndhjem, and take a ride by cariole through the country for about one hundred and fifty miles, and intercept the steamer at Namsos. We started a day ahead of her leaving Throndhjem, and took the cars for sixteen miles, to a station with the euphonious name of "Hell." We crossed a river which might be the "Styx," but there was no "old ferryman there to ferry us over the river Styx," and they have a bridge now. We passed safely, and a boy pointed out to us the first cariole station, or *skyds*, as it is called in Norwegian.

Almost every town in Norway is reached by steamboats, and there are no stages or conveyances through the country. The government has, therefore, created a system of "posting," as they call it, by cariole (at a cost of about six to eight cents per mile), which is a kind of gig, like a race-horse vehicle, only it is ugly and clumsy in appearance. It has two long poles and a prow-shaped body, and a seat like a half bowl, just large enough for one person to sit on. The feet must rest on a cross-piece, directly in the rear of the horse. Behind is a board, on the ends of the poles, to strap the luggage onto, while the "gut," (boy) or "pige," (girl) takes a seat, with legs dangling, and keeps one company till the next station, when they take back the cariole.

There are no springs to this primitive conveyance, and one can imagine the jolting when a stone or a hole obstructs the progress. The harness is equally primitive ; no blinders, with rope lines and a small piece of board each side for the iron saddle-tree to rest on. The horse draws by the poles, with a kind of wooden fastening attached to the harness. You are yourself expected to drive.

The roads are made by the government,

and the whole distance of one hundred and fifty miles was as smooth as the roadway in any well-kept park. The stations are from five to eight miles apart, and each is a farmhouse, where they are obliged to have two or three horses, according to the amount of travel, always in readiness. These are the farm horses, and in one instance were taken from the mowing machine for our use. The farmer is liable to a fine if he keeps one waiting more than fifteen to thirty minutes, and it is often a great detriment to his business.

At the second station we drove up to no one came to the door (so it was at every station), and we had to find our way into the room where the traveler is expected to register his name in the "sydsbog," or day-book, and the number of horses he wants, and any complaints he has to make in regard to his treatment, delay, etc. In the front of the book are found the laws, passed by the Parliament, imposing the fines, etc., for not complying with the law and fixing the duty, etc. An inspector comes along at stated times and makes an examination, and if anything is wrong the law is very arbitrary.

We waited at one station an hour for our horses to come; they were off in the field, some distance, at work : if the farmers have not the horses at home they are obliged to procure them from the neighboring farmers ; we thought with such delay as this our steamer would not wait for us, and with over one hundred miles to drive, the prospect of meeting our friends was not very encouraging; we started, however, with very good speed, as the ponies were fresh, we soon came to a gate across the road and a boy jumped off quickly, and opened it, and, although we started the horse as soon as possible the boy jumped on and we went on at a John Gilpen speed, though every few miles was another gate to open.

We learned that each landholder has a gate across the road at the entrance and exit to his premises which gives the "skydsgut" plenty to do in opening and closing them.

During the entire one hundred and fifty miles we did not meet ten carioles or vehicles ; we saw scarcely any one on the road or about the farm-houses, and only saw men and women in the hay-fields cutting the grass and making the hay by putting it on poles to dry.

There were large farm-houses with several barns, the former painted white or yellow, the latter red, in every direction overlooking the beautiful valleys, the farmers always choosing an elevated and commanding position; the buildings are made of logs and covered with boards, two stories in height, and stretching out at great length ; there is generally the living-house in front for the family, on one side the servants " or tenants," on the other side the barn, and on the third side the store-house for butter and milk, all of which from a hollow square ; there are no cellars under the houses.

The dwellings are plainly furnished—no carpets, but the floors are covered with sprigs of juniper, which emit a pleasant odor and everything is clean and neat. In one house was a sewing-machine and a woman spinning wool into yarn, and the farmer at work with his mowing machine out doors, the only one we saw the whole distance, Around the rooms are generally some very common wood engravings of Christ, Luther, the Prodigal Son in his different stages; Norway's great poet, Bjornsterne-Bjorson, and some of the radical leaders.

The peasants are all radical and are prejudiced against kings and an aristocracy, and in favor of a republican form of government.

They have a good education, and are a plain, frugal, industrious people, kind and unconventional, sit down to table with their servants, and each one is expected to help himself without ceremony.

We picked up a little Norwegian language, which seemed to help us much, as they have a horror about being ordered to do anything, and at the changes when I wanted anything I would say "Vaer saa gud strax," (be so good at once as to do so and so), and they would run off at once, and we had no more delays in changing horses.

At the third station I had a "pige" (girl) for my "skyds," and she tried to be very social, but as I could not understand a word she said, except as she would say "America" and point to different farm-houses, I judged that from the houses some or all of their inmates had emigrated to America; she said in broken English, "I would like to go." When I told them I was from America, they would brighten up and say "I have a broder (brother) and a soster (sister) in America," and asked me, "Do you know my broder in San Francisco? Do you know my soster in Mobile?" Having no idea of our country of such magnificent distances.

The large emigration from Norway and Sweden, which amounted to one thousand per week last year, is alarming the government, and they are doing all they can to prevent it, our courier says "that our government won't long hold together, on account of the southern, northern and western interests being antagonistic ; and warns the young men if they go to America they will probably get into a war. Such warnings don't have any effect, as the news comes from those who have gone to America of their success. We met quite a number who were now on a visit to this country ; they were mostly from Minnesota. They like the climate of the north-west—it is more like their own.

The country through which we passed on our long drive of one hundred and fifty miles, was well cultivated. They raise rye, barley, oats and potatoes ; but toward the north end, for fifty miles, nothing but white birch and Norway spruce trees and hazel bushes were seen. All along the road were beautiful flowers, heath, cornel, loosestrife golden rod, queen of the meadow, bluebell, stone-crops (several varieties), orchids, flowering sedge, white daisy, buttercups, several species of pyzola, creeping vetch and many

other common flowers and plants. One of
the most beautiful is a long creeping plant,
with small, nearly round opposite leaves, and
two tiny, pinkish flowers hanging together
from an upright stalk ; it is called *Linnæa
borealis*, and is peculiar to Norway and
Sweden. The name has been adopted as the
emblem of the great Linnæus, the world-
renowned Swedish botanist. Its low, trailing
habit and late bloom are considered typical
of Linnæus' humble origin and late fame.
We found all these plants, and many more,
on our way to North Cape Mountain. It
would seem as if the season was too short
for plants to bloom in latitude seventy-one
minutes, ten degrees north, but the sun
shining for nearly three months brings vegetation forward most rapidly.

The first day we had ridden seventy miles
in our unsocial carioles over hill and dale,
through forests of pine, besides lakes and
fjords, with such diversified scenery that we
had forgotten how tired we were, and then
the sun did not go down until ten-thirty, but
at eleven o'clock we were glad to stop for the
night, and take the remainder of our journey
the next day.

We reached Namsos in time to go aboard

of our steamer, after waiting two or three hours for it to come in. These were "red-letter" days for us. We had not had much to eat but milk and dry wafer-like bread, made of rye and oatmeal, in large, round thin cakes, as much as a foot in circumference, and piled up in the " starbur " (storehouse) five or six feet high, and, when it is to be eaten, it can be broken into all kinds of shapes, as it is so brittle. This is the only kind of bread they have, and but little can be eaten at once.

Everywhere, on the steamer or in the towns, the Norwegians are ready to do one a favor, or answer questions when they can speak English, as most of the officers on the steamboats can, and at the hotels ; and the Government officials, whom one meets, will point out this mountain, that glacier, or some beautiful view, and repeat some legend connected with the spot. One gentleman from Christiana, who traveled with us nearly the whole distance, was so exceedingly kind and intelligent that he won all our hearts. He expected to meet us on our return, but was disappointed, and sent us by telegraph the following message :

" Nordland, over thy silent waters, through

thy ever-lighted air, thou unfoldest for the traveler's wondering sight thy magic, lofty panorama, pointing to heaven ; there springs forth the pure the root on earth, the crown in heaven. May we meet there. God bless you all, and may He carry you safe and saved to your distant homes.

"Yours truly,   C. NIELSEN."

This shows the kindess of the people. At Tromso a gentleman went a long distance out of his way to show me the post-office. One of the girls on the cariole, at the end of the route, when I gave her a small sum of money, as is customary to the one who accompanies you, shook hands with me several times ; such is the custom when they receive a gift.

One would judge that most of the boys are named Olaf or Oscar, and they seem to worship Saint Olaf. On our cariole ride through the country, we found the boy had directed us out of our way about six miles to Stiktesad. The view was most beautiful, and all at once the boy pointed to a monument and stopped the horse. There was a well-trod path to an ornamented fence surrounding a monument erected to the memory of Saint Olaf, who fell in the famous battle in the annals of Norway, July 29th, 1030. There is also a beautiful church erected to his memory near the spot where he was killed, and everybody visiting the neighborhood goes to this monument; many Norwegians make a pilgrimage to it, so the boy took it for granted that we also wanted to go there. We did not care anything for Saint Olaf, and we did not like to be taken out of our way six miles at that time of night, when we had twenty-five miles farther to go.

Our journey by steamer, with the small state-rooms, and many other inconveniences, would have been tedious enough but for the magnificent scenery, the delightful weather, the winds, the play of the light and shade, the purity of the atmosphere—all quite unlike the natural features that we have anywhere seen either in Europe or America. The waters seem to be full of fish—whales, cod, herring, salmon, and many others, which are the source of immense revenue to Norway. The long line of warehouses at the landings in every place are to store fish, and all over the rocks, in many places, they are packing or drying fish; and long lines of girls can be seen unloading codfish from the vessels, passing the fish from one to the other, others spreading them out on the rocks to dry, and others piling them up in round piles, over which are placed dome-shaped coverings when the weather is wet.

There seems to be an infinity of birds. Swan, geese, pelicans, grebe ducks, auk ducks, gulls, etc. The eider duck is a great curiosity. We brought away an eider down quilt, which is quite curious to our friends, as it is made of the skins of the male eider duck.

Our tour through Norway was a great success. There was so much that was grand, picturesque, new to us and exciting. It culminated in our journey, by cariole, through the far-famed valleys of the Romsdal and Gudbrandsdal, over two hundred miles. The cariole I have already described as peculiar to Norway.

IV.

MOLDE. A NATIVE WEDDING. THE BEAUTIES OF NATURE. CHURCH AT LISTAD.

WE started from Throndhjem by steamer to Molde, one of the most beautiful towns in Norway. Our attention was continually attracted by the most beautiful roses and rare flowers in every yard, and in the windows of all the dwellings, both of the rich and the poor. The valley is so sheltered by hills and mountains that vegetation is unusually luxurious, and such roses and honeysuckles running over the houses in the middle of August we have never seen.

There was a grand wedding in the church the day we were there. The daughter of the sheriff was married, and all the flags were flying from the vessels, and from almost every house, and from the villas on the mountain sides, the young ladies were out on the streets in their gayest attire. Roses and flowers were taken to the church in great profusion, and a more beautiful scene we have never witnessed.

Everywhere in Scandinavia we notice that the fine dwellings and public buildings have a flagstaff, and on all public occasions the people run up the union-jack and the flag of their nation, which gives a gay appearance ; and to this is added the display of flags in the harbor, where each vessel runs up the colors of it nationality.

The views from the mountains are the most picturesque in Norway. The Romsdalhorn, and the long range of peculiar shaped mountains covered with snow, the lakes and fjords, with the Atlantic ocean stretching out to the west, make a charming picture. This place has become so attractive, by reason of its scenery, fishing and hunting, that a large hotel is to be erected here the coming season, to accommodate the numerous tourists.

We leave this place by steamer on the Romsdal fjord, winding our way out into the open sea until we enter the fjord. The ride the entire distance is most enchanting, with the high mountains ranging from five to six thousand feet, covered with snow and glaciers, and on the side of the fjord, nestling in among the hills, the beautiful white and red farm-houses and out-buildings, and an occasional kirke (church) on an eminence, the green hillsides and valleys, quite in contrast with the bare rocks along the Norwegian coast, that we have been looking at in our journey to the North Cape.

We arrive at Veblungsnaes, at the head of the fjord, amidst a heavy rainstorm, and find our carioles in waiting, and, as they are not covered, we get wet through on our ride to Aak, the first station, where we are glad to stay over night, and dry our clothing by the huge kitchen fireplace. After supper at this old unique hotel, we all go out to get a view of the Romsdalhorn, usually known as the Horn, which is over five thousand feet high, with a horn-shaped rock running up into the air over eight hundred feet from the top of the mountain. In every direction are large mountains, over six thousand feet high, and covered with snow. All at once the sun comes out, and throws its light over the distant heights and on the green hillsides, various shades of green, gold and silver, with a rainbow spanning the whole, enchants us, and we all stand in admiration of this never-to-be-forgotten sunset at the Aak Hotel under the mountains.

A LAP HUT.

Some of the ladies of our party are sketching the scene, but it is impossible to put in the continual beautiful lights and shades which we have noticed are peculiar to Norway. The young landlord at our hotel keeps us awake late telling of his numerous experiences with Englishmen, while with them as guide on their hunting and fishing excursions. He is a good story-teller, and his peculiar voice and broken English, and exciting manner, short, stubby appearance, with his long pipe in his mouth, are laughable enough.

We are up early in the morning for our three or four days' ride by cariole through the most interesting part of Norway—along the Rauma and Lagen Valleys, known as the Romsdal and Gudbransdal. The morning was a delightful one, the sun clear, and the air cool and bracing after the rain of the night before. We soon rode along under the lofty Romsdalhorn, extending perpendicularly on one side of us, and the rapid Rausna, full of cataracts and waterfalls, on the other. The ride that day, and the novel, picturesque scenes during a walk of eight or ten miles, will not soon be effaced from our memory. Some one calls this the valley of one thousand waterfalls; some of them drop over precipices more than two thousand feet high. The walls of the gulley below have been worn into deep caldrons by the action of the water, which nearly disappears in spray before it reaches the bottom, where its roar is loudly reverberated. The whole drive is one continued succession of surprises, with lofty mountains and small houses along the valley, white birches and alders by the road side, and luxuriant pastures on the slopes of the hills.

Some of our party seemed to think this valley equal to the Yosemite in California, but to me it does not appear so grand and imposing, and not so picturesque as some parts of Switzerland; but it is peculiar to itself, and well pays one fond of such scenery to visit it.

We leave this valley, after a journey of forty or fifty miles, and come to the Gudbransdal Valley, which is tame in comparison, but the ride gives us an opportunity to see the peasantry and their farms, and peculiar dress and mode of living. These cariole rides are not recommended for their speed, as one is likely to meet with many drawbacks from want of horses and the dilatory manner of the keepers at the stations, where we were detained sometimes for two or three hours. Only four or five horses are available at each station, and if some one happens to be in advance of you, you are obliged to wait until the horses come back from the station beyond, and then they have to be rested and fed. Thus, instead of two days, as promised, we were three and one-half days from Aak to Lillehammer, and experienced many ludicrous scenes. Our meals were usually good, as trout is abundant, and we had it at almost every meal ; the bread of rye and oats was thin as a wafer, hard and brittle.

At Domars we stayed several hours ; it is on a high hill, and the air is fresh and invigorating ; this point is at the junction of the Gudbrandsdal, Dorufjeld and Throndhjem routes. Here we met three American young ladies traveling alone, or rather with only a courier ; we were surprised at their independence for ladies so young ; they had been to the North Cape, and were going to spend the summer in Norway. In conversation, we found the youngest not over fourteen or fifteen years of age ; we were interested in seeing them pack themselves away in their carioles, and drive off one after the other over the route we had just traveled.

Our experience at the next station was not an agreeable one, although the station master claimed his descent from the first King of Norway in 1030, "Harold Haanfagre," and showed us several crowns, one of the old King's and another a bride's silver crown, and a number of old curiosities; this man was so displeased because one of our English bloods came into the station on a canter, that he would not allow us to have the horses for an hour, and then only by coaxing and a promise from the young man that he should go behind us.

It is delightful to notice how kind all the Norwegians are to their horses; every little while the boy or girl who attends us will stop them and step around to stroke their faces and look over them to see if they are sweating. Going up hill they also stop them and let them get wind—this young Englishman caused us a great deal of trouble on account of his fast driving, as the word was passed along by the (skydot gut) boy to the other stations to look out for him.

This is a historic valley and our intelligent driver (Olaf Ees), who was valuable to us as a courier, although he could speak hardly a word of English, was so bright that he managed to learn a good many words of us and we of him—it is easy to do this, as there are many words in Norwegian and English that are similar—pointed out to us many historical spots; one was a mountain precipice where three hundred Norwegian peasants hurled down huge stones upon nine hundred Scotch troops, in 1612, and killed nearly every one of them, including Colonel Sinclair, the commander.

The troops had just landed and were pillaging and robbing the peasants, and endeavoring to force their way through Norway to join the Swedes; a tablet in the rock commemorates the deed as follows: " Erindring om Bondernes Tappered." A little further on is a stone to show where Colonel Sinclair was buried.

In the neighborhood we were shown the (gaard steig) farm-house, where the leader of the peasants who annihilated the Scottish invaders lived; near here is also the seat of Dale Gudbrand, the powerful heathen opponent of Saint Olaf, and the scene of heathen sacrificial rites.

On Sunday we attended church (kirke) at

Listad ; the church is an old octagon, built in 1720, it is in a quaint style of architecture, with a tower in the centre, which is painted black ; inside were galleries all around the building. When I entered I heard a voice reading or praying, and looked around to see where it came from, and for some time supposed it was some one hid from view, but, finally looking up, saw the priest perched upon a high pulpit far above the audience. He looked as if he might be the old reformer Luther himself, with his long gown and Elizabethian collar and ruffle around his neck.

The peasants are very plainly dressed, the women wearing white handkerchiefs around their necks and on their head ; barely one had on a bonnet, and they looked queer enough, as they would bow their heads and then raise them again, all over the church. Most all of the attendants were women. A number brought their babes to have them baptized. The priests are highly educated, and much venerated by the peasants, who speak lovingly of their self-sacrificing devotion to them during the long and cold winter nights, going from place to place over the mountains to minister to their necessities.

The priests have small salaries, but connected with each church is a (proestgaad) parsonage, with a farm attached, which is cultivated under the direction of the priest. The building is usually an imposing farmhouse and out-buildings, the former painted white, the latter red. The young people at the station were preparing for a grand tea party, for a Sunday night entertainment, which they enjoyed hugely.

These valleys are spoken of as highly cultivated, but to us the farms looked small, and many of the houses inferior, and hardly any cattle to be seen. The driver thought that the cattle were off to the saeters, a pasture place on the mountains, where the stock is sent for the summer, and cared for by the girls of the farm, generally living in little huts, and returned to the farms when the snow comes in the fall.

We passed continually waterfalls, and to-day we had too many falls over our heads, or, rather, on our heads, and had no protection but our waterproof garments, which, however, proved equal to the situation. We stopped to look at the Hunnerfos, a splendid fall, spreading out over a great surface, with numerous rapids.

We were glad to reach Lillihammer, the end of our cariole journey of three and one-half days, tired and wet enough, and were glad to continue our journey by steamer, on the beautiful Lake Mjoesen, the longest in Norway, being sixty-three miles in length. On each side are beautiful farm-houses and green hillsides, and the scenery quite in contrast with what we have been witnessing for the past three or four weeks. At the end of the lake we take railroad for the beautiful city of Christiana, the capital of Norway, where we spend a few days most agreeably, visiting the various places of interest, among them the "exposition" for Scandinavia, which is now in progress. Here we do not find much of interest, only what is peculiar to the northern countries. Some of the paintings in the art gallery are quite creditable, especially those of some of the beautiful fjords and fishing towns we had visited. We were glad to see that some of the finest were by Mr. Normann, a Norwegian artist, with whom we had traveled to the North Cape. He was continually taking sketches, and it seems to me, no country in the world abounds in such grand scenery for the artist's pencil.

The American consul, to whom I was

favored with a letter of introduction, was very attentive to us, and accompanied us through Oscar Hall, and pointed out to us the beautiful scenery around Christiana, and invited us to his lovely villa, a short distance from the city, where he has a farm of one hundred and fifty acres adjoining. The buildings are extensive, and of an old style of Norwegian architecture, of which I was anxious to obtain a photograph, they were so quaint. The grounds are laid out in the old English style of parks and lakes. The consul's wife is an American lady. He is a Norwegian, and I wish all our consuls were so worthy of their position. He rendered us much valuable service in obtaining information for shipping goods to America, and about the laws and customs of the country.

Norway is greatly excited, politically, now, and a great impeachment trial is going on in Christiana, in the Parliament buildings, before the highest court. It seems the King, Oscar II., vetoed some bill, passed by the Parliament, and the ministry and counsellors confirmed it, and the country became so aroused about their rights being interfered with, that they have undertaken to impeach them. We were in the court, but could not understand a word. The names of the eleven were handed to us, as printed and lying on the desks of the impeaching court.

The peasants of Norway are republicans, and are quite radical in their views, and are jealous of any infringement upon their rights. The inhabitants of the cities are, on the other hand, conservative. We could not quite understand the controversy, but by the excited discussions on the steamboats, and the pamphlets scattered over the country, we judged the excitement to be at fever heat.

One of the leading papers here published a review of Colonel Robert Ingersoll's lectures on the Bible, and in the review printed long extracts from his works, and for this the paper has been summoned before the court of Norway for "blasphemy," and this is also creating a great deal of discussion, some of the leading papers taking the ground that it is interfering with the freedom of the press, others that it is a dangerous, unlawful document to print.

V.

THE KING AND HIS REALM. DESPOTISM TOWARD SENTIMENT. NORWAY AND SWEDEN CONTRASTED.

OSCAR II. is King over Norway and Sweden, and yet the two nations do not seem to have anything else in common; they are only united for defense. Their language, habits and laws are distinct. Even in passing from Norway to Sweden we had to undergo an examination of our baggage, showing that duties are charged on certain articles passing from one country to the other. The King lives most of the time in Stockholm, and the people of Norway are jealous of it. He comes to Christiana, according to law, when Parliament convenes in September, but only remains as long as he is obliged to, in order to carry out the law. The King is much liked by the aristocracy, and seems really to be a man of ability and culture. The American Consul informed us that a literary association offered a premium for the best Scandinavian poem. The committee who were to decide were not to know the authors of the different poems, and when they selected the poem they considered the best, they found the author was King Oscar II., which much pleased his admirers and the aristocracy.

When I asked the peasants, "Why do you not have a republic in Norway, you are largely in the majority?" they replied, "We would not be allowed to be a republic, other nations would interfere." The situation in Norway is becoming daily more serious ; the impeachment trial of the ministers, just concluded, has had the effect of irritating the King. The late premier, whom the Supreme Court of the kingdom sentenced to loss of office and a heavy fine, is rewarded with the Serafimer Cross, the highest distinction for civic merit ; and another minister, who was also fined and censured by the same tribunal, has been appointed chief of a new cabinet. All the other lately appointed ministers are extreme conservatives.

Every editor, whether in Norway or Sweden, who has the courage to criticize the King's conduct with any degree of spirit, is unceremoniously thrown into jail, preliminary to trial for offending his Majesty. With the utmost nonchalance this same Majesty, however, writes a letter, or so-called dictamen, expressing his opinion of the Norwegian Parliament, and the highest tribunal of Norway, and it is superfluous to remark that his opinion is highly uncomplimentary; but when Bjorstjerne Bjornson in turn expresses an equally uncomplimentary opinion of the dictamen, its royal author responds by trying the editor who has published Bjornson's letter for *crimen laesae majestatis.* Bjornson, who has been living in Paris during the last year, as soon as the intelligence reached him, took the first train for the North, and has now arrived in Norway, and declared his purpose to assume the responsibility for his own words. Probably he has been imprisoned, though no intelligence to that effect has yet reached us. Intense excitement is reigning throughout the country, and everybody asks his neighbor, with bated breath, "What will happen next?" That Bjornson will be tried is inevitable, and the chances are that in that trial the Government will be sowing the crop of dragon-teeth which sooner or later will sprout forth in armed men.

Some of the most valuable farms in Norway would be spurned as a gift by American husbandmen, who are seldom content with places of sudden undulation, or indeed, with anything but pieces of rich prairie or bottom land. But the Norwegians are industrious and thrifty grangers, have comfortable barns and fine cattle, and generations of families succeed each other in possessing and working their mountain farmsteads. Their houses are substantially constructed of wood, and inside there is an air of comfort and cleanliness. But what of the farm? "Look about you," says Chambers' Journal, "mountains hem us in on all sides; there is no room for fields as we know them at home; but grass grows luxuriantly among the rocks, with occasionally a patch as large as an ordinary villa garden; there the farmer cuts a portion of his hay crop on which his horses and cattle are mainly dependent during the eight winter months. But his hay field is yet wider spread. Glance upwards some fifteen hundred feet there, where an opening occurs in the dwarf birch, and you will observe the diminished form of a man busy at work. That is the farmer, a thorough mountaineer, cutting the grass which grows on yonder narrow ledge of rock. He has been up since early morn, and will probably not descend till evening. Not a tuft of grass will be left ungathered; not a foot of level ground on that steep and rugged mountain side but will be visited, and its small crop carefully removed by the industrious bergsman. If he has a wide stretch of field (hill pasture or moorland) in his boundary, the farmer erects wooden sheds, in which he stores his hay till winter, when, by an ingenious contrivance, he has the whole rapidly and easily conveyed to the valley. A familiar object in a Norwegian glen is the strong steel wire which stretches from the foot to the summit of the mountain. Down this wire the bundles of hay are expeditiously sent without labor, and then carried in sledges to the steadings. Without such a method many weary journeys would be necessary ere the hay required for a long winter could be brought down. It appears the Norwegian farmer borrowed the idea of his hay telegraph from his brother hillsmen of the Tyrol about eight years ago. The hay crop is the product of natural grass, no seed being sown nor any admixture of clover being used.

Norway presents us with the grandest picture of the effects of peasant proprietorship; there the land has, from time immemorial, been the property of the laborer who tills it—it has never been poisoned by the foul curse of feudalism. The title deeds of these peasant holdings are in a dead language, and the names of the peasants are those of the district; the results are marvellous. Land which no English or American farmer would or could cultivate under our agricultural system, even if receiving a liberal bounty per acre instead of paying rent, is there made to support whole families, and that by the same race as ourselves and in latitudes hundreds of miles further north, some of it even within the Arctic circle.

Sailing along the coast of Norway the tourist passes here and there little oases, called "stations," where the steam omnibus halts to land and embark a passenger or two. If a careful observer, he may learn that in the midst of the rocky desolation there is a deposit of rock fragments and gravel left by an ancient glacier in a hollow formerly filled by the ice. This is cultivated, is a dairy farm and fishing station, farmers and fishers being all freeholders and capitalists, no such class as laborers without property existing there.

One of the grandest of the Norwegian fjords is the Geiranger; it is walled by perpendicu-

IN THE LAND OF THE MIDNIGHT SUN.

lar precipices from one thousand to three thousand feet high. Sailing along the fjord, a boathouse is seen here and there at the foot of the dark wall. Looking skyward directly above it may be seen what appear to be toy houses on a green patch; closer observations reveals moving objects; a field-glass shows that they are cattle, goats, and children, tethered to bowlders to prevent them from straying over the edge of the precipice. A family resides up there, cultivating this bit of ancient ground, backed by craggy mountain tops, with a foreground of precipice above the fjord. The only cummunication between these eagle-nest farmers and the outer world is by the boat below; how the boat is reached, where is the staircase of ledges on the face of the precipice, is incomprehensible to the passing tourist; in most cases no indication of a track is visible. Nothing but absolute proprietorship by the cultivator could bring such land into cultivation—latitute sixty-two degrees, altitude two thousand to three thousand feet; summer only three to four months long; the ground covered with snow during six to eight months of every year—requires a race such as we found the Norwegians to be: intelligent, kind, frugal and industrious.

The five hundred thousand of them now in our own country, and more coming in every year, will be welcomed as the right kind of citizens to make good republicans, and the more that come the better.

We had the good luck to witness a very interesting ceremonial—namely, a village wedding, when about fifty persons assembled, all in their holiday costume—the women in bright-colored petticoats and bodices, with beautiful white chemisettes. They were a very pleasant looking group—the men strong, well-knit fellows, but all fair-skinned, with flaxen hair and kind blue eyes.

The bride was a demure young woman, somewhat overweighted with necklaces and bracelets (which we understood to be heirlooms), but more especially by an immense gilt crown running up in tall points to a height of about eight inches, and studded with many colored crystals. It was a most gorgeous head-dress, and belongs to the village.

Every village is supposed to have one, which is hired for the occasion by the parents of the bride. But, like the plain ribbon or snood of the Scottish highland maid, no Norwegian bride is entitled to wear this crown of honor unless her character is above suspicion ;

and this, unhappily, is so very exceptional, that the hiring of the crown is now considered almost invidious on the part of the few who may certainly claim it ; so the custom is dying out, and we esteemed ourselves fortunate in having witnessed a nuptial cermony in which this picturesque bridal decoration was worn.

There was no architectural beauty in the very plain, barn-like church, which had no pretense at decoration. The Lutheran service, which, of course, was conducted in Norwegian, seemed to us like that of the Scotch Presbyterian church. All the men sat on one side and the women on the other, according to the usual custom. The parson, in his black gown and white fluted collar, performed the simple service, in which a wedding ring shaped like a double heart did duty in place of our plain circlet. He then ascended the pulpit and delivered a very long exhortation which, being beyond our comprehension, was to us only suggestive of Longfellow's charming lines :—

> "Long was the good man's sermon,
> Yet it seemed not long to me
> For he spake of Ruth the beautiful,
> And still I thought of thee."

There was one feature in the ceremony which we noted with especial interest, therein recognizing a lingering trace of pre-Christian days. The pulpit stands in the centre of a large chancel, and, at a pause in the service, all the wedding party walked solemnly thrice around it, in sidewise procession—a pretty revival of old Norse paganism.

Any one with an observing eye cannot but notice a great difference between Norway and Sweden, while visiting the two countries, although under one king, Oscar II., who is a Swede. The relation between the two countries does not seem to be cordial, and I should not be surprised if there should be, before many years, a permanent breach. The constitutions are quite different, that of Norway being more democratic in its character than that of the sister kingdom, and the people of the former seem more democratic, and do not worship the king, as many seem to do in Sweden. There have been, however, great changes in the Constitution of Sweden since 1860, under Oscar I., who was exceedingly popular, and the Constitution of Sweden has been brought more into harmony with that of Norway, with its two Chambers, both now elective.

In visiting the half dozen splendid palaces, maintained by the two governments for the king, four in Sweden and two in Norway, one can not but wonder that intelligent people could be satisfied at the immense expense it involves to keep up royalty. With a population of only about five million (two million in Norway, and three million in Sweden) these great palaces are kept up just to support the king's family. The cost of the palaces, and maintaining of the king's household, no doubt is more than it costs to maintain all the great benevolent and educational institutions and hospitals in any one State of the United States.

I took note of what I saw in the palaces, and the beautiful grounds and hunting parks attached to them, but to go into the details of what I saw would be only a repetition of what has already been described in other countries. Gold and silver dining sets, the most expensive paintings and statuary, Sevres ware, and gobelin tapestry, and furniture of the most expensive nature, are not too good for each of the six palaces of the King of Sweden and Norway.

In traveling through the two countries we did not see school-houses scattered along the country, as in the United States, and on inquiry of our courier, I learn that the schools in the country are held in the farm-houses. Education in Sweden and Norway is compulsory, all children being required to attend school who cannot satisfy the authorities that they are receiving sufficient education at home.

In Sweden places of instruction are divided into three kinds, the *folkskolor*, or "people's schools," answering to our public schools; all *mannaskolor*, "public schools," which are to be found in all the larger towns, and the universities. All of these are under the control of the ecclesiastical (and educational) department, and partly under the bishops and clergy of the diocese to which they belong.

The State churches are Lutheran. The religious instruction is entirely under the management of the pastor. The minimum of subjects taught before a pupil can leave school and be *confirmed*, are reading, writing, arithmetic, church catechism, Bible history and singing. But the higher branches are also taught. Besides these, popular schools of a more advanced kind, called *folkhogskolor*, designed to give a higher culture to the laboring classes, are being established in different parts of the country. To each of the higher schools a library is attached. In all schools botany is taught in the lower classes. The bishop of each diocese seems to have control of, or is supervisor, of the schools in the diocese, and he appoints an inspector for each school.

Great importance is attached to gymnastic exercises throughout Sweden, both as a means of giving a healthy physique, and also as a remedy against certain kinds of bodily ailment. For such purposes the *Gymnastika Centralinstiut* was founded by Per Henzik Ling, the great inventor of Swedish gymnastics. This establishment is divided into three departments. One to train officers to superintend gymnastics in the army and navy. A second to train teachers of gymnastics for the town and country schools, and a third for the study of gymnastics as a system of medical treatment. The system has been adopted with more or less success in Germany, England, and other countries.

We visited the great university at Upsala, with its one thousand two hundred students, about forty or fifty miles from Stockholm. This is considered the historical and intellectual centre of the kingdom to which it belongs. Anciently it also formed the stronghold of Paganism, memorials of which abound in the tombs and monuments of the neighborhood. The town looked old, and does not have the appearance of life and thrift. The old cathedral is the first object that attracts attention. It was begun in the year 1260, and finished in 1435. It is built upon the site of the old heathen temple, Upsala, an edifice spoken of in the early Saga legends to have been of enormous size and immense wealth.

We were here more interested to see the place where the great Linnæus was buried in the cathedral than to see the tombs of the Kings of Sweden. We were shown the place where Linnæus lived; we see the evidences of his genius in the great botanical institution built here in connection with the college herbarium, fine floral collection and many rare plants, although in latitude of more than sixty degrees. There is a fine building in the gardens, with a good statue of Linnæus in a sitting posture with a book, on which is the little flower called *Linnæa borealis*, which has been adopted as the emblem of the great botanist. We saw this flower in the pine forests in the north of Norway, and picked a quantity of it to bring home with us. Linnæus is called, by the Swedes " The King of Flowers." He was the first one to perfect anything like a systematic and scientific manner of classification of plants and animals.

In the library we see the famous *Codex Argentus*, a translation of the four gospels into Maeso Gothic by Bishop Uphilas, dating from the fourth century, written on one hundred and eighty-eight leaves of parchment, in gold and silver letters, on a reddish ground—this was captured in the thirty years' war. We are shown here the three great mounds, or burial places, from the bronze age. They are attributed to the heathen gods Odin, Thor and Frey, whence we have Onsday (Wednesday), Thorsday (Thursday), Freyday (Friday). These mounds look very much like the mounds seen in many of the Middle and Western States, and are interesting as suggesting the sources of our names for the days of the week. The highest mound, sixty-four feet, was cut through in 1864, to enable the Universal Ethnographical Congress, that met in Upsala, to examine the inside of it. Fragments of a skeleton and some ornaments were found.

Hundreds of smaller mounds can be seen for miles around.

Stockholm is one of the most beautiful cities in Europe, and has a population of one hundred and seventy-five thousand to two hundred thousand. The situation of it on islands, on a plain and on rocky hills, surrounded by water and numerous islands in almost every direction, makes it exceedingly picturesque, and it is well called the "Venice of the North." From the Belvidere and the top of the elevator one is astonished at the lovely panorama of the city, and its forest of trees and rocks which surround it; Lake Malar, with the beautiful islands covered with verdure, the summer villas of the wealthy citizens, and the fifty steamers plying in every direction; the Baltic at our feet, with its busy traffic, all presents a scene of unrivalled beauty and attractiveness.

We are glad to have Sunday come, and to take a day of rest, for this sight-seeing keeps one busy with body and mind. We attended service at the cathedral, and at the Katharina Kyaka, founded in 1609, on the spot where the victims of the "Stockholm Bloodbath," of 1389, had been interred, where a large number of burghers had been cruelly murdered.

We notice the priests in Sweden do not wear the Elizabethian collar as in Norway. The services seemed to us just like those of the Roman Catholic church; the priest before the altar in his scarlet and gold vestments, and the ringing of the little bells and turning his face to the altar, with his back to the audience, and many other things gave it the appearance of a Catholic rather than a Lutheran church.

We expected to hear splendid music in the city of Jennie Lind and Christina Nillsson, who have so charmed us by their wonderful voices; no one has ever seemed to me to equal Jennie Lind in the bird-like sweetness of her voice. But the music in the churches has slow, minor tones, and nothing especially to note in the voices in any of the churches which we attended. Near this church is the house where Swedenborg, the celebrated mathematician, philosopher and author of the New Jerusalem church doctrines, lived; our guide informed us that there are none of his followers in Sweden, but that an Englishman (there are many of those who follow his religious system in England) purchased the little summer house that was in the garden, and took it to England.

All about the city, on the islands, where one goes by steamer, are gardens, and one hears most delightful music. On Sunday evening there were great crowds of people at King Park, in the center of the city, to hear the music and to promenade ; opposite our hotel near the palace, on the River Nord, which runs rapidly between Lake Malar and the Baltic, is a garden where every night is music and we found this a most attractive place.

Our ride by steamer to Drottingholm Palace on Lake Malar, a lake about eighty miles long, with over one thousand two hundred islands on which are many beautiful villas, the summer residences of the wealthy citizens of Stockholm, was an enchanting one. The palace was built in the sixteenth century and contains many sumptuously furnished apartments and paintings, and the grounds are laid out in the old French style with sculpture in bronze and marble.

There seems to be something new to see in Stockholm every day, and our time there seemed altogether too short, and we put this city down as a place to visit again. The picture gallery in the museum building contains many works of art by the old masters, but we were glad to turn our attention to those of the Swedish school which represent landscape, fjord, lake and mountain scenery by Tidemand, whose paintings in Oscar Hall, in Christiana, around the dining-room near the ceiling and representing the "Seven Ages of Peasant Life," certainly indicate that he is one of the best artists in Scandinavia ; and his paintings here, where there are quite a number, show great genius as an artist, and the people are proud of him ; our consul at Christiana thinks he is superior to any other Swedish artist.

I have before remarked that they have adopted in Norway and Sweden the "Gottenborg system" of regulating the liquor traffic ; it is sold to what is called a Temperance Company, who must pay all profits into the municipality, and no one is allowed to sell who has any interest in the profits. Or a city or a district may refuse to sell liquor at retail. Liquor shops are closed in the country, and in town may be closed by the authorities, on Sunday and holidays. Stockholm adopted the "Gottenborg system" in 1877, and the police statistics show that drunkenness and crime are steadily decreasing.

At the tables, at hotels and private houses,

they have a liquor called pomaraine, a kind of "schnaaps," and most of the gentlemen and ladies drink a small wine-glass full before eating, which they say is an appetizer. It is villainous tasting stuff with a flavor like chloroform and is made of potatoes. They have a curious custom before each meal; a decanter of this liquor is placed on a side table with all kinds of cold meat and fish, and the guests are invited into the dining-room, each one steps up and takes a glass of liquor and helps himself to the cold meats, then walks around the room or out of doors and chats for awhile before he is invited to sit down to a regular warm meal. Some of the party, not understanding this custom, made the full meal on the cold viands, not knowing that they were merely an introduction, or appetizer as they call it.

VI.

ACROSS THE BALTIC TO FINLAND. THE CHARACTER OF THE FINS.

OUR ride across the Baltic Sea, from Stockholm to Finland was one of the most charming of our tour; the scenery, for forty miles, until you reach the open sea, is one of continued picturesque islands, and on each side are more of the beautiful villas of the wealthy citizens of Stockholm.

After a good night's sleep and a smooth sea, we find ourselves in the morning winding our way among the innumerable Aland Islands; the sailing is intricate and dangerous, but picturesque; we are obliged to stop nights on account of the danger and difficulty in navigating among the rocks.

The Gulf of Finland, which we enter, is in possession of Russia; by occupying the Aland Islands she is only twenty miles from Stockholm, and is, therefore, brought into close proximity to Sweden. Our passengers on the steamer are mostly Fins and a few

Russians, and a more intelligent class of people than the former we never met; they were evidently from the higher classes, and one of the young ladies was reported to be the belle of the capital of Finland. Of the party, a prominent lawyer and a member of the Senate, could speak a little English, and they gave us much valuable information.

Russians are quite jealous of the privileges granted by the Emperor Alexander I. to Finland on the conquest of the country, and these have been further guaranteed by succeeding Emperors; they have a Senate of their own, composed of two hundred members, belonging to four orders—nobility, clergy, elected by the clergy and professors of colleges; the industrial interests representing the large towns and cities, and the peasants representing the farmers. It is necessary that all or a majority agree in passing any law, and no troops can be raised without their consent; in the Crimean war only about five hundred troops were from Finland, just enough to say to the Emperor that she was represented; they have their own army and navy, educational and postal systems.

The Emperor of Russia is not called Empe-

A LAPLANDER'S HUT

.ror of Finland, but Grand Duke of Finland. The population is over two million; they are mostly Protestants (Lutherans), and they are obliged to teach their own language and not the Russian in their schools; indeed they are allowed a kind of local self-government. They do not like Russia, but with Russia "might makes right," and they cannot help themselves, as Russia feels the importance of controlling the Baltic, and until her surrender to Peter the Great, in 1809, Finland was fighting the ground between Russia and Sweden continually.

We stop at Abo, the former capital of Finland, which was removed to Helsingfors on account of her people being wanting in loyalty to Russia. We had been warned to have our passports "vised" by the Russian Consul at Berlin, and to be doubly prepared, we had it done also before leaving Stockholm; at Abo, a number of Russian custom-officers came on board the steamer and took our passports, and examined closely our baggage, but in a gentlemanly manner, quite in contrast with some of our New York custom-house officers.

No person is allowed to go in or out of Russia, not even her own citizens, without a passport; the officers examined every nook and corner of the steamer, taking the bed-clothes from the berths and looking under them; the captain informed us that he is subject to a heavy fine if any one is found on the steamer without a passport.

We got into a "drosky," a peculiar low kind of a vehicle, for a drive about the city, and especially to visit the old cathedral. Abo is the most ancient city in Finland and has a population of over twenty-five thousand, not a large number for a city that dates from the twelfth century, when Christianity was first introduced into this wild and cold region. The cathedral of "Saint Henriks" is not interesting architecturally, but historically; it was the cradle of Christianity in Finland; the vaults of the chapels are like the Catacombs and are filled with the remains of the early distinguished families. On one of the monuments is an epitaph to "Catherina Mansdotten," a girl taken from the ranks of the people by Eric XIV., in the twelfth century, and who, after having won the Swedish diadem, returned to Finland and died in obscurity, while her royal husband ended his days in prison.

There is a beautiful stained window in the

chapel, representing the Queen Catherina, leaving her glory and grandeur, which she bequeaths to Sweden, and descending the steps to the throne, with her hand affectionately placed on the shoulders of a page, which typifies Finland. The other page, of whom she appears to be taking leave, representing Sweden. Many ancient monuments are here, but the most interesting, the bones of Saint Henriks, have been removed to Saint Petersburg. There is here an old castle, built in the thirteenth century, and other objects of interest. We ascend the observatory in the botanical gardens, and get a fine view of the beautiful city and surrounding country.

VII.

ST. PETERSBURG, THE GREAT CAPITAL. SIGHTS OF INTEREST. THE PALACE AND FORTRESSES.

WE can hardly realize that we are in this great city of a million population, founded by Peter the Great, in 1703. Some one describes St. Petersburg as "the eye by which Russia looks upon Europe." It is built on both banks of the Neva, and on several islands, which one can see from the cupola of St. Isaac in a clear day. Fourteen rivers and streams, and eight canals, intersect the city in various parts. It was the design of Peter the Great to build the city on the north side of the Neva, formerly belonging to Sweden, which was taken by him from Sweden, but his councillors advised a different course, as Sweden might win back her possessions, and he would lose his city.

Everywhere one sees relics of this wonderful man. Our second day in St. Petersburg was a holiday—"Transfiguration day"—and we concluded to spend our time in visiting the churches, and witnessing the services, and seeing the people. Our hotel is on St. Isaac's square. Our rooms front the grand old cathedral of St. Isaac, and we never tire of admiring its grand proportions of " modified Byzantine " simple and lofty style of architecture.

All the ground about St. Petersburg is flat and uninteresting, but the situation of the cathedral is on one of the largest squares, and is surrounded by lofty, splendid buildings, which give to it an imposing appearance. It is remarkable how different from most of the Greek churches it is, with hardly an ornament, built of stone from the Finland granite quarries. There are one hundred and twelve pillars, sixty feet high and seven feet in diameter. Over the main building is the central cupola, about three hundred feet high, supported by thirty pillars of polished granite. The cupola is covered with gold, and on the top ball is a golden cross, three hundred and thirty-six feet above the ground. One hundred and eighty-five pounds of gold cover the cupola, not including the cross. The interior of the church is grand and gorgeous in the extreme, with its different colored malachite colums and lapis lazuli pillars. The floor and walls are of polished marble from the Russian quarries in Siberia. All the beautiful paintings on the walls are by Russian artists. The gilding is profuse, as in all Greek churches. We were glad to be located near it, that we may often visit it, and get a view of the city after ascending nearly five hundred and fifty steps. It was commenced by Catherine II., but half completed by Paul. One Russian writer paid the penalty of exile to Siberia by saying, "This church is a symbol of *three* reigns, granite, brick and destruction." One notices, on entering a Greek church, large piles of candles, which are being sold to every one that comes in, who light them and go up to the altar, or pass them up through the crowd of worshippers, to be placed in one of the holes in a large silver stand, after crossing his breast a number of times with the thumb and two forefingers of his right hand and falling on his knees before the altar. His prayers are short, and he goes out with his face to the altar, kneeling and crossing himself. They seem to think the offering of a lighted candle has some miraculous power which saves them from their sins. I understand the sale of wax candles is a source of large income to the church. We saw a babe in the mother's arms placing a candle in its place and crossing itself under its mother's instructions. "Flame with the worshippers is a symbol of the continued life of the good."

Every one in these crowded churches to-day, men, women and children, seemed so sad and devotional, that one could not but feel that this was true devotion to their Maker according to their knowledge. There are no sacred ceremonies, no marriage, no burial, and no baptism without a light, either lamp or wax candle, and illuminations are a great feature in Russian churches.

There are no organs or musical instruments in their churches, and all the voices are male. We never listened to such grand, harmonious music, as we heard in the Russian churches. We were told that the choicest music was at the "Monastery of St. Alexander Nevsky," one of the most noted in Russia, and for its building and decoration Peter the Great expended immense sums. The marble was brought from foreign countries, the precious stones from Siberia, and pearls in abundance. Paintings from Rubens, and other of the old masters, adorn the walls. The shrine of Alexander Nevsky is of silver, and weighs nearly thirty-five thousand pounds. Over it are silver angels as large as life, with silver trumpets, as everywhere there are life-size portraits of Peter the Great and Catharine II. The archbishop officiated to-day, and the ceremony was extremely gorgeous with the gold and silver wardrobes of the archbishop and priests. On one side of the altar were thirty-five monks, and opposite thirty-five boy singers. The bishop would intone the prayers, and one side would respond and then the other, and following altogether. The bishop was very large, with a rich, heavy bass voice, and we never heard such soprano and alto voices from any, however, as these monks possessed. The harmony was like the rich tones of an organ, rising to the grandest sounds, and falling to the minor, soft, sweet tones of the organ. There did not seem to be many voices, but one voice. We never experienced such thrilling delight in music. The bishop seemed to be preparing for sacrament, and the unleavened cakes were borne on a silver altar by six priests through the cathedral, followed by a procession of priests, and the altar placed on the floor, where the carpet, or rug, had been prepared for it, and the singers all marched down singing ; and

RUSSIAN VILLAGE AND PEASANTS.

after various performances and burning of incense, and swinging silver incense lamps, they return to the main altar, after stopping at different places, once directly in front of us, and the singing was continued until the end of the service. All of the service by the voice was intoning or singing.

The church is a fashionable one, and the Emperor is sometimes present. They show you in the cloister an immense number of gold staffs, pearls and precious stones, and the bed on which Peter died.

We visit the "Preobrajenski," or fortress church, adorned within and without with trophies from conquered nations. We found the greatest crowd of people here, outside and in, and we could hardly push our way through, so great was the mass of human beings, all peasants or common people, with the peculiar dress of the women, with red bodices and red handkerchiefs on their heads. We soon learned the cause of the crowd. Alexander II.'s uniform and sword, with spots of blood upon it, which he wore when assassinated, were exposed to view in a silver case, and the people lingered around it as if the Czar had just been killed. I understand the people never weary of looking at them and stopping at the beautiful chapel erected where the bombs exploded and the Czar was killed. Even shrines are in the railroad stations with a picture of him, which the people worship. Evidently the common people are loyal to the autocratic power, and they do not forget that Alexander II. saved more men from slavery than any other human being by the emancipation of twenty-two million of serfs in 1861, giving them their liberty. The Nihilists evidently do not come from this class, but, as our intelligent guide said, from the nobles who had their means of support taken from them by the emancipation act. They were accustomed to hire out their serfs and received a large income from that source, and the enemies of the government are in its own household. The lower classes, our guide informed us, would almost take the life of any one heard saying anything against the Czar.

Sunday was as quiet and orderly a day in St. Petersburg as in any city in the world, and the churches in the morning were crowded with people, and the great bells, one weighing sixty-four thousand pounds, of St. Isaac's, and the numerous other bells awakened us with their melodious silvery sounds.

We went to St. Isaac's Cathedral and heard a sermon. By the attention given by the great audience standing (there are no seats in the Russian churches), we have no doubt they were deeply interested, and there must have been an immense sale of wax candles from the number burning around the church.

We went from there to the English Episcopal Church, and found a small audience and heard an impotent sermon that we could understand. We enjoyed the singing and services in our own language.

We witnessed a number of funerals on the street, some with pall-bearers dressed in black, bearing the corps on their shoulders, followed by a little family, weeping, on foot, and other funerel processions with the hearse covered with gold and silver trappings and white plumes and silver harness upon the splendid large black horses, with a retinue of splendid carriages. One thing was noticeable—that when a funeral procession passes, no matter who they were, all take off their hats and stop a minute. It is wonderful how the people of all classes, high and low, rich and poor, seem to worship the Czar and the church, as they are one with them.

VIII.

THE FAMOUS CATHEDRALS. FOUNDLING HOSPITALS. VERITABLY "A CITY OF PALACES."

A LARGE cathedral is to be erected on the spot where the Czar was assassinated, and twelve million rubles had already been raised for that purpose. Among the other cathedrals we visited was the Kazan, dedicated to our Lady of Kazan. It is built after the style of St. Peter's of Rome. Diamonds and precious stones of the most costly and exquisite beauty are seen everywhere; but the silver case contained, as the priest showed us, the genuine right hand of "John the Baptist," a piece of "the Holy Cross of our Saviour," "a Picture of Saint Luke," taken from life, "a piece of the shirt of our Saviour," and a miraculous image of the Virgin, brought from Kazan in 1579, covered with fine gold and precious stones, valued at one hundred thousand dollars. There are a great many churches here, and it would tire the reader to follow us with all of interest that we saw.

Another great crowd was at Peter the Great's cottage, which was the first house and cottage he built in 1703. A great many things, including the celebrated boat of Peter the Great, which he built and sailed himself, having served as an apprentice to a ship-builder. The great crowd seemed to be pushing their way to a little chapel which was formerly used for his dining-room. Candles were sold and lighted, and carried to the altar, and we are informed that all Russians leaving St. Petersburg on a journey, come here and make an offering to the miraculous image of the saviour which accompanied Peter the Great in his battles, and assisted at the battle of "Poltava." They believe if they do this that prosperity during their journey and a safe return will be vouchsafed to them. When the Russians are in great trouble they go to St. Isaac's Cathedral, and when they desire "business prosperity" to accompany them, they go to the Kazan Cathedral. If in sickness they go to the Preobrajenski Church; if to be married, to St. Peter and St. Paul, and buy a candle and place it on the altar and make an offering. All these add largely to the coffers of the church finances. In the church of St. Peter and St. Paul, with the highest spires in Russia, three hundred and seventy-one feet high, all the Emperors have been buried since the foundation of St. Petersburg. Alexander II. and his wife are buried here and a great number gather about his sarcophagus, which is covered continually with wreaths of flowers brought from different parts of the empire. Near him is that of his wife with a beautiful memorial in marble in a reclining posture with an angel over her weeping. We bought a copy of a memorial printed in Russian, with fine portraits of both.

We notice about the Russian churches a large number of beggars with their plates in their hands, holding them out to receive benefactions. A beggar with them is still regarded as almost a holy person, and they are voluminous in their pious vows and benedictions for a person who gives them anything.

"The Foundling Hospital" is the most interesting institution, founded by Catherine II. We were first shown by the good matron to the window on the street where each infant is received into the hospital, and it is not necessarily known who brought it or where it came from. A register was shown us where these questions only are asked: "Has the child been baptized? What name?" The child then has a number placed against the name, which is worn around its neck and on its bed, when a receipt is handed to the bearer of the child, and the mother can visit it if she chooses, or claim it after ten years. We visited the different wards, one room where twenty-five had been brought in that morning, and were being bathed and dressed, and wet-nurses (the latter all dressed in check dresses and white bodices and bare arms) assigned to them. Most of these nurses were young peasant girls, who probably had children in the institution unknown to the manager. Many of them had two children nursing at the same time. We were shown into fifteen or twenty different departments, and everything was clean and neat, and every exertion possible made to preserve life. In one room a large number were prematurely born, and the manager informed us that they nearly all die. The warm bathing-rooms, and the dressing of the little things in white linen swaddling clothes on down pillows, was as delicately and tenderly performed as if they were the children of the rich. In most of the rooms as we entered all the nurses would stand up with the babes in their arms. One room was shown us containing a dozen or more dead ones being prepared for burial, another room where baths and other appliances were used to fan the flame of life apparently almost extinct. It is said the number is increasing rapidly, and about ten thousand are admitted annually, and about fifty per cent. die before they reach the age of one year, as after remaining for four weeks, and having been vaccinated, they are sent to the villages where the nurses formerly lived. Only about twenty-five per cent. of those brought to the institution arrive at maturity. The nurses get about one dollar a month for nursing and caring for them. About thirty thousand in all have been cared for in the adjacent villages, factories, etc.

The official who showed us through the building was exceedingly polite and attentive, and had upon his breast a number of gold medals received for bravery in numerous battles in which he had participated, and at our request he gave us the names of the battles, but I do not remember. Some of them were in the Crimean war, and he was on the retired list, serving the government in this way. A marble statue of Betski, the projector, an eminent philanthropist, and a portrait of Catherine II. adorn the walls of the entrance hall.

When Russia undertakes any enterprise like this, or, indeed, anything else, she seems to have "Excelsior" for her motto. Some argue that such institutions increase illegitimacy, and that there are a larger number of illegitimate births in Russia than France. No doubt there is some other reason for this than the humane care for the unfortunate babies. Our ladies called my attention to the care given to a large number prematurely brought into the world, and discussed the humanity of trying to save those who, to them, seemed never could become strong and of good constitutions, even if kept alive. In a double box, about two feet long, stuffed and cushioned with down, were two little red faces, about the size of the palm of the hand, peeping through the soft downy caps, all shriveled and drawn up. You could only see the faces. Outside the box, and between the bodies, was warm water, creating a warm vaporous atmosphere, and if anything would keep the little waifs alive this care and kind attention would put life into them.

At night we witnessed a scene quite in contrast. We visited one of the great public gardens, some distance from the center of the city, called the Zoölogical Gardens, lighted with electric light, where are a large number of wild animals of all descriptions, and beautiful grounds with shady trees and flower-beds, and various performances, operatic, where was some splendid Russian singing, a band of music and gymnastic exercises, comic singing, and everything to amuse the masses.

We had quite an experience with our drosky drivers in getting to the garden. A drosky is a small, low, four-wheeled vehicle, and it was necessary to place my arms around my wife to keep her from falling out, the seat was so narrow. Five or six droskies started off from our hotel together, "Jehu" like, but soon they got into a race in spite of all we could do. On they went, passing every one on the way at a breakneck speed, which would have amused our American friends. All we had do was to hold our breath and hold on to our seat. Our driver came out ahead and as the others came following on they did not care to have another drosky race. We had a wild babel scene at the entrance gate, for we had made a contract with our drivers to take us to the garden for a certain sum, and when we came to pay them they demanded more, I suppose on account of the race. We could not understand a word of the Russian language, and they could not understand us, and they swung their whips and gesticulated until the police came, and we were glad to get off by paying what they demanded. The harnesses have a curious appendage; over the shoulders of the horse is a kind of inverted wooden ox-bow three or four feet high. Some are painted green and some fancy figures of saints. I cannot understand the object and it seems as if it was merely an old custom which they cling to. One of our gentlemen thought it was artistic, but to me they seem a heavy, unnecessary appendage which adds to the burden of the horse. There is not more than one-quarter of the leather in their harnesses as with us, and they are light and graceful.

The drosky drivers in the hottest days are all dressed in a long plaited woolen frock reaching to the feet, with a band around the waist and a regulation cap, which gives them the appearance of a priest in his long garments. It seems as if they must be heavy, cumbersome and uncomfortable, and why they should be required to dress thus I could not understand. In wet and muddy weather the garments, all filth, draggle around their feet.

"The city of Palaces." I asked our intelligent guide. "How many different palaces has the Czar?" He replied, "Fifteen or twenty," and some of them, like the winter palace, the largest and most magnificent in the world, with its one hundred and twenty-eight magnificently furnished rooms, the winter residence of the Emperor. We are told that since the assassination of the late Emperor no one but the family are allowed to visit the winter palace. After considerable trouble and efforts of our guide, who said our being Americans helped him in getting permission from the commissioners, we gained admission. He said Americans were held in high esteem by the government.

We were delighted with the prospect and gave one day to the winter palace and hermitage. We were surprised at its immense size as we approached it from the Neva. It is about four hundred and fifty feet long by three hundred and fifty feet in breadth and eighty feet high. We pass through room after room and various halls, covered mostly with battle scenes and portraits of Emperors and Queens and distinguished persons.

We have visited most of the palaces in Europe and have never seen anything to compare with the drawing-rooms of the Empress, with the gold-covered walls and ceilings, and when illuminited at evening receptions must present an enchanting scene. We were not allowed to see the crown jewels, as three days before they had been sealed up according to custom after a coronation, and would not be opened for three years. We passed through the Emperor's (Alexander II.) dining-room, which was blown up just as he was about entering in 1881, killing eighteen soldiers. In one minute more he would have been blown to atoms. The steps under which the fuse was placed were lifted from their places and blown to pieces, and the rooms in the vicinity more or less shattered. All the gold and precious stones of the Ural mountains could not insure his life, and he was at last assassinated.

The rooms and bed where the late Empress died, and was kept alive for six months by artificial means after life seemed extinct; an ox was killed every day and the warm blood put into her bath-tub and she was kept alive by bathing in it. These rooms are to be closed and not opened to the public for a generation. The present Empress' rooms were splendid. She is the daughter of the King of Denmark and sister of the Princess of Wales of England, and is said to be the most intelligent and best posted Queen in the world in regard to the affairs of government; but how unhappy and anxious she must be amid all the glittering jewels and silver and golden wardrobe and richest lace around her bed. We then come to the room where Emperor Nicholas died in 1855, on a plain iron bedstead, and cheaply furnished apartments. The room, with his cloak and garments, just as he left it, with all the appurtenances, report of the quartermaster, etc., just as it was when he heard of the defeat of his army in the Crimea. He was so overwhelmed with disappointment that he died suddenly on receiving the news.

On every article in the room is a pocket handkerchief. One of his peculiarities was an extravagant use of pocket handkerchiefs, and he had one on everything in the room where it could be within his reach.

We visited the Hermitage gallery of paintings adjoining the palace, founded by Catharine II., who gave its name "Hermitage." It forms a parallelogram five hundred and fifty feet by about four hundred, and for its splendid architectural proportions and costly marbles is the finest gallery in the world, and contains about two thousand paintings. Among some of the most valuable of the masters are sixty of Rubens, including portraits of his first and second wives, and many others of great value; twenty by Murillo, including "The Assumption;" many of Raphael's, VanDyck's, Tenier's, Paul Potter's and Titian's. The Hermitage has more paintings by Rembrandt than all of Holland, where he lived. One can never tire of looking at these wonderful works of art by the best artists of Holland, Germany, Italy. France, England and Russia, which we found here.

The numismatic collection, commenced by Catherine II., is perhaps the largest in the world, with its eight thousand specimens of Russian coins, some dating from the tenth century. There are over two hundred thousand specimens in these rooms, and we were more interested with the one thousand specimens or more of Etheldred II., Canute and other early kings of England, which have been found in Russia, where they must have been circulated in payment for the celebrated furs of Russia. The collection of gems and precious stones is almost without number, and one gets confused with the immense number and value of these specimens of vases, mosaic tables, etc.

Peter the Great's room is one of the most attractive, containing a large number of the various specimens of his mechanical genius, where we see his engravings, turning and carpenter work, as he not only ruled a great empire, but worked as a mechanic, and the telescope and mathematical instruments which he used are seen, and a wooden rod is shown us of his height, which measured seven feet, a large number of portraits in oil and statuary and an effigy in the peculiar odd dress of the time in which he lived, embroidered for him by Catherine I. for her coronation. We see everywhere something to remind us of Peter the Great.

All Russia seems but one vast monument of his genius. "He gave her six new provinces, a footing upon two seas, a regular army trained on the Europeon system, a large fleet, an admiralty, and a naval academy, educational establishments, and this splendid

FARM LIFE IN NORTH RUSSIA.

gallery of painting and sculpture and library. Nothing seemed to escape his notice. He had the Russian letters altered to make them adapted to printing, and changed the dress of his subjects to be more in conformity with the rest of Europe," and all this was accomplished in a lifetime of only a half century, as he died at the age of fifty-two. His son, Alexis, no doubt came to his sudden death through the instrumentality of his father, and he no doubt had many intrigues with ladies of his court, showing traces that "the hero was mixed with much clay." Forcing his wife, Eudoxia, to take the veil and transferred his affections to others, and finally married Catherine, the daughter of a peasant and wife of a Swedish corporal, whose family had been taken prisoners. She was said to be an amiable but illiterate woman, who could neither read or write. She succeeded Peter the Great, receiving the homage of her courtiers in the room in the winter palace (where we are) while the body of Peter was lying in state. The Russians never weary of showing you something about him at nearly every place we visited. At Peterhof is a low Dutch looking summer house where he lived, and where Empress Elizabeth used to cook her own dinners in the great fire-place. His various rooms with paintings which he purchased while traveling in Holland ; his bed, night-cap, dressing-gown and slippers, etc. They tell an incident that occurred while he was on a visit to London. While going to Westminster hall he noticed a large number of men with wigs and gowns on. Peter asked who those people might be? and when informed by those accompanying him that they were lawyers. "Lawyers!" he said. "Why I have but two in all my dominions and I believe I shall have one of them hung when I get home."

IX.

THE MINING SCHOOL. MUSEUMS AND ACADE-
MIES. PETERHOF. DANGERS FROM NIHILISM.

WE visited the celebrated mining school, which is one of the most complete in the world. The superintendent gave each one of us a lighted taper, and we went under ground, and apparently through mountains, in various directions, for a long distance, and the different geological positions of the minerals as they are found in the Ural mountains, with layers and color of the different minerals of coal, platina, iron, copper, silver, gold and precious stones, sapphires, emerald, amethyst, agate, rhodorite, the rock crystal, jasper, chrysoberyl, and black tourmaline and diamonds. All was explained to us, and I could well understand how a student would have a complete knowledge of mining with such practical illustrations and applications. There are about three hundred pupils, and miners are represented in miniature, going through the operations of mining, and we could hardly realize that we were not examining genuine mines. There are here, perhaps, the best collection of minerals in the world. A solid piece of real gold, from Siberia, worth fifty millions of rubles, an immense number of pearls, some as large as a walnut, the largest in the world. The mineral wealth of Russia is immense. The specimens of beryls, tourmalines, topazes, and other precious stones from Siberia are astonishing. Some of the beryls were a foot in length, large tourquois, and the largest black diamond in the world, a solid mass of malachite, weighing thirty cwt. One becomes confused at the splendid display of minerals and precious stones.

There seems to be no end to academies of sciences and museums in St. Petersburg. In the Zoölogical Museum the great mastodon and rhinoceros, the largest, I am told, in the world, found on the banks of the river Lena, in Siberia, by a peasant. These had been preserved (we are told) one hundred thousand years, or countless ages, in the ice of Siberian rivers, and the flesh so preserved that, when discovered, wolves and bears came down to feed upon them. This frame, as it was put together, looked to us, as near as we could measure it, thirteen to fifteen feet long, and two feet higher than a large elephant in the vicinity. Its tusks were eight to ten feet long.

After examining numerous museums, galleries of paintings, palaces, etc., our guide remarked, "all these belong to the Emperor. He has the key to the government treasury. The people have nothing!"

Our visit to Peterhof, the present residence of Alexander III., was intensely interesting, as the Emperor and his family were here. We were fortunate in having a most delightful day. We took the steamer down the Neva, and across the gulf of Finland, about twenty miles. We could see Cronstadt in the distance, and the beautiful palaces of Peterhof peeping through the green forests. On board our steamer were a number of officers of the Russian army and their families, dressed as they all seemed to be everywhere, with heavy cadet mixed overcoats, reaching to their feet. No matter how warm it is (this was a warm August day) they wear their heavy overcoats. While we were talking with our guide, who was a Russian, I noticed a number of police in uniform standing around us, and slyly creeping up behind us, evidently to hear what we were talking about, and soon two ladies, who could talk English, came near to us, and remained until we changed our location, and then, as if by chance, appeared near us again, and were about when we were on deck, or in the cabin, both going and returning. We were conversing with our guide about the Czar, mentioning his name frequently, and asking questions about the family, and the guide was pointing out to me the villa where he resided, etc. The guide suddenly whispered to me that we must cease talking about the Emperor, as the police heard us mentioning the name of Alexander III. frequently, and they were gathering around us to learn what we were saying; and the two ladies were private detectives, who accompany every steamer and watch every stranger to see if they can discover if any one has designs on the Emperor. Ever since the coronation unusual precaution is used. We did nòt feel very comfortable in a strange country, and only Mrs. S. and myself, to have so many of the police and detectives about us. Everybody seems to look at each other in Russia ominously, and ask "What is going to happen next?" The coronation is over. Much excitement followed the publication of the rescript of the

Czar. All seemed to think in Russia that after the coronation every kind of business would revive; all who were poor would be rich; all who were in prison would be free; all the exiles in Siberia would be liberated; all foreigners were to become naturalized, or leave the country, and refused a passport to remain. The Nihilists expected a constitution. It has now been three months since the coronation and nothing is done. The Emperor announces that nothing will be done. Business in St. Petersburg is unsettled, and the government is using every effort to prevent another assassination. When we arrived at the wharf at Peterhof, a number of splendid equipages were in waiting for the officers of the army. One general entered a small open Victoria phaeton, drawn by four splendid horses abreast, and a number of others followed.

Our approach to the grounds was enchanting. The palaces were plain style of architecture, built by Peter the Great in 1720, on rising ground about sixty or seventy feet. As we approach them we look through the long arches of trees and in the distance see fountains playing in every direction, until we reach the fountain called the Samson, tearing open the jaws of a lion, out of which the water rushes. In front of the palace is a waterfall probably one hundred feet high, falling over wide steps, behind which are colored lamps, placed behind the water for an illumination. Over one hundred jets of water were playing eighty to one hundred feet high, and one foot in diameter. From the top of the steps we have a view to the sea, five hundred yards, through the forests where a river runs, and the gardens laid out in terraces and flowers, fountains and waterfalls; the Lion Fountain, the Neptunes, storks, nymphs, dolphins, rocks and grottoes; with the water thrown in every direction—all seems like fairyland. We think the magnificence and artistic arrangement superior to those at Versailles, or any in the world, and we were fortunate in visiting here on a day when they were all playing. It was a gala day, and great crowds of the elite of St. Petersburg were here with their splendid equipages. Not less than one hundred carriages were in a row, while their occupants were promenading up and down the beautiful grounds. On each side were bands of music—one would play and then the other, and in the distance others could be heard. The dresses of the ladies were equal to any we ever saw in Paris, rich, but in good taste. The ladies were large and fair-looking, with a German look. When I learned afterward that nearly one-half of the population of St. Petersburg were Germans, accounted for the appearance of the ladies. We visited the palaces and villas, which are scattered through the grounds, adorned with lakes and flower gardens, and the chalets belonging to the royal family. One especially, belonging to the late Emperor Nicholas' wife, finished in blue with mosaic floors and tables, captivated my wife.

The most attractive paintings in the palace were, I should think, nine hundred or one thousand portraits of beautiful Russian girls from the different provinces of Russia in the peculiar costumes of their country, in different positions, with all the colors of their wardrobes, with a different expression and position to each one, one leaning over a chair as if listening to a lover, etc.

After spending the day here we could not but cast a glance and a thought at the poor Emperor and his family in their Alexandrian villa, with a high wall around the premises, and numerous soldiers guarding the walls and entrance and not allowing any one, not even the servants, to go in or out without a pass, and when he comes from or goes to the city, his steamer lands far away from the other landings, near his villa. We met a black steamer bearing dispatches to him from the Premier de Girs, who informs him what is going on in his own dominions and in the world, twice a day. This was a grand day for us, and we came away with the impression that Peterhof was more beautiful than Hampton Court, Versailles, Schonbrunn in Vienna, or Potsdam in Berlin. On our return to the steamer we found the same lady detectives and police, but Mrs. S. did not enjoy being under police surveillance in Russia.

While we were there we understood that Nihilist papers were being distributed in the Emperor's palace among his own household. One day the Empress opened the door suddenly into the chamberlain's room, and she observed that he hid a paper away in his side pocket. She had him examined, and the paper proved to be a Nihilist paper, and without any trial he was summarily sent to Siberia. There are a great many arrests made every few days, but it seems to be the policy of the government to keep it from the people, and the papers say that all is peace and harmony.

X.

MOSCOW. THE CAPITAL OF THE RURIKS. THE TOWN OF IVAN. THE GREAT BELL. THE PEASANTRY AND THEIR CHARACTER.

OUR ride from St. Petersburg to Moscow by rail was an interesting one, over a splendid road, with compartment cars, which are arranged for very comfortable sleeping cars. All the appurtenances of the road are first-class; the road is straight and solid, and the depots are large, built of stone, and of attractive style of architecture. At the end of the depot is a bell over which is a roof covered with woodbine, which hangs gracefully down to the ground. There are three bells of warning sounded before the cars start, followed by blowing of the engine whistle. It is stated that when the engineer of the road presented his profile and plans to build the road, showing how each large city could be reached, the Emperor was dissatisfied, and took out his rule and drew a straight line from St. Petersburg to Moscow, and said, "Build the road straight, without regard to cities or obstacles." It was done, and branch roads had to be constructed to accommodate the cities, but he had an opportunity to show his autocratic power.

Our first view of "Matushka Moskva," Mother Moskva, as the peasants delight to call the capital of the Ruriks, was early one beautiful morning, from our car of observation from St. Petersburg, just as the bright sun shone out upon the eight hundred churches; many of them, with their towers and turrets covered with gold, gave a most thrilling feeling as we for the first time looked upon the city with so many historical associations. There is a great contrast between this city and St. Petersburg—the latter with its wide, straight streets, and splendid modern architectural buildings, all of stone or brick, covered with stucco of a yellowish tint, the surface of the country flat and uninteresting, looks like a modern city like Chicago; while Moscow is on hills, with sudden ascents and descents, with winding streets, and many of the houses are frame, and the roofs are painted green, and it looks like an oriental city. The most prominent thing is its antique churches of the showy, gaudy Byzantine architecture, with five towers or spires. All of the Greek churches formerly had seven towers, but Peter the Great issued the "ukase" that the churches should have only five. Moscow is Russian, and you see that it is Asiatic, while St. Petersburg is European. On the streets we at once noticed the bright red dresses and scarlet handkerchiefs of the women, pinned coquettishly on the head, and the red cotton shirts or smock frocks, fastened around the waist by a girdle, of the working men. We begin to realize that we are in an ancient city, built first in the twelfth century, and several times destroyed by fire—the last time at the entrance of Napoleon in 1812—and for many years the capital of Russia. It is a prosperous and growing city of about seven hundred thousand inhabitants, and when you ask, what are your business prospects? the answer is quite in contrast with the reply in St. Petersburg: "All our numerous manufactories, about six hundred in all, employing fifty thousand men; are in operation, and there is a good demand for all our products. This is the great center of the Russian railway system, and we expect to be a larger city than our rival on the Neva. Why should we not, with our central location and Russia's one hundred million population, and increasing?" We certainly have not seen more activity in the streets of any city that we have visited. The Kremlin has been the great palladium of Russia, and is regarded with superstitious veneration. We first take a carriage to ride about the city, and get the best view of the Kremlin, which is a triangular inclosure of about two miles, situated on the Moskva River, and a ride along the river under the Kremlin gives one an idea of the oriental and picturesque hill, surrounded with high, strong walls, with its thirty-two churches, and the only part of Moscow which was saved from the terrible conflagration in 1812. We enter the Kremlin first through the Redeemer's gate (there are five gates in all built in the fifteenth century). As we passed through the gate we noticed a number of women on each side bowing to the ground and crossing themselves, looking directly toward us, and we took off our hats and bowed to them, when we were informed that we were not the object of their attention, but the picture of the Redeemer of Smolensk, held in high veneration. We were unfortunate in having a drunken driver who could hardly sit upon the seat; but he did not forget to bow and cross himself several times, and remind us that we were passing through the holy gate, and that we must take off our hats, as the Emperor and every one else was expected to do. We desired to conform to the old custom and tradition, and uncovered our heads.

We first prepare to ascend the great "tower of Ivan the Great," three hundred and twenty-five feet high, erected in 1600. We stop to look at the largest bell in the world, called "Tzar Kolokol," king of bells, which lies at the foot of the tower on a pedestal, and weighs four hundred and forty-four thousand pounds, is twenty-six feet high, and sixty-eight feet in circumference. The tower is five stories high, and we counted in it thirty-four bells, the largest, with the name of the "Assumption" on it, weighing sixty-four tons. On the top of the tower we get a splendid view of Moscow, and it is certainly one of the most wonderful and unique cities in the world. The Kremlin is below us, the Moskva winding its way through the city, with the numerous boats upon it, and a great number of women in their bright dresses washing in the river. The splendid churches, with their gold and silver domes glittering in the sunshine, the roofs of the houses all painted green, and the distant hills from which Napoleon first looked upon the city in flames, after his long march in mid-winter, all come rushing into one's mind with the historical incidents connected with the terrible march. There is a chapel in the lower part of the tower, which was especially interesting to the young ladies, and is called St. Nicholas, where the young ladies of Moscow all go who are about to marry, as St. Nicholas is their patron saint. Near by is the cathedral of the Assumption, with its five domes, which is more of Saxon and Norman style of architecture than Italian, and was consecrated in 1479. This cathedral is especially interesting as being the church where all the Emperors are crowned, and where the present Czar was crowned last May (twenty-seven old style, or fifteen new style), or rather crowned himself, as he places the crown upon his head with his own hands. The platform was carpeted where he stood, and the pictures of one thousand saints on the walls covered with gold, all of which had been burnished up for the coronation.

Among the very old and valuable paintings is one which they say was painted by St.

NORTH RUSSIANS.

Luke, of the Holy Virgin. A small case is opened, and we are shown a nail of the Cross of Christ and a piece of his robe and various other old relics of the Apostles, which they seem to believe are genuine, but this does not prevent us doubting it. These cathedrals contain so many articles and rich vases studded with diamonds and precious stones, as if the rich mineral resources of Russia had been exhausted to adorn the churches. Near this cathedral is that of St. Michael's, where all the Russian Czars were buried until the time of Peter the Great. It is similar in architectural appearance to the former and was built in the fourteenth century, and was the place where Napoleon stabled his horses in 1812. The tomb of the greatest interest is that of Ivan, "The Terrible," who forms the subject of so many Russian poems. Special funeral services are held here twice a year, with great pomp, where the souls of all those who are buried here are prayed for by the church. The priest allowed the gentlemen of the party (no ladies were allowed inside the "Ikonostas") to examine the gorgeous vestments and costly treasures which had been presented to the church to pay for prayers being offered up for the souls of departed friends,

A cross which belonged to Ivan, "The Terrible," had immense pearls in it, and an emerald one-third to one-half an inch in diameter. We were interested most in a splendid illuminated version of the Gospels with the date 1125—the earliest copy in Russia; the cover was enameled and full of the most rare and costly precious stones. Another church near there is that of the Annunciation, where all the Czars are baptized and married. Here also are shown a great many relics, one an image of the Holy Virgin, made of three hundred and sixty pounds of silver and twenty pounds of gold, brought from Constantinople five hundred years ago, and was often carried in the early battles of Russia, and was considered to have miraculous power. There are a great many curious frescoes here, and the floor of the church is paved with agate and jasper. These three cathedrals adjoining each other are historic on account of that of the Assumption being where the Czars are crowned, St. Michael's where they are buried, and the Annunciation where they are baptized and married. The place is also shown where the false Demetrius fell while leaping from one of the windows behind the palace.

Near the entrance to the Kremlin by the

Spankoi gate is one of the most curious fantastic churches in the world, which is called St. Basil, and was built in 1554, by Ivan, "The Terrible." It has fifteen towers and the same number of chapels inside, and is painted outside with a variety of bright colors, green predominating, and the architect, so it is stated, had his eyes put out by Ivan so that he could not build another church like it. Napoleon ordered it destroyed, but it was saved. We never shall forget that on the day we visited it some fifty or seventy-five bright boys came in and most devoutly were offering their devotions in a solemn and graceful manner. As they enter the chapel they drop on to one knee, bowing the head to the pavement, crossing the breast frequently with the thumb and two fore-fingers of the right hand ; as they return they kneel and cross themselves. The boys were so bright and all dressed in linen suits, with white caps and closely cut hair, that I asked our guide who they were. The superintendent, who was with them, informed me that they were from the deaf and dumb school. I was glad to meet him, and we conversed awhile as best we could through an interpreter, and he gave me a cordial invitation to visit the school at three o'clock p. m. All the scholars in schools for the deaf and dumb in Russia are taught to speak, and no instruction is given by signs whatever. There are similar schools in St. Petersburg and in Warsaw, which we visited. They claim that every deaf mute can be taught to talk, and all the instruction is given orally.

The new cathedral, called St. Saviour, is one of the most conspicuous in Moscow, and was dedicated just after the coronation in May last, and was commenced by Alexander I. forty-two years ago, in commemoration of Russia's delivery from the French. It is of stone and Byzantine style of architecture. The architect was sick at the time it was to be dedicated, and he asked to be taken to it so that he could survey his splendid architectural production, and died a day or two afterward, before it was dedicated. There are about six thousand paintings, of various historical and allegorical scenes and saints, and cost fifteen millions of rubles or about six million dollars. When illuminated, as it was at the dedication, twelve thousand candles were lighted, so arranged about the inside as to present a most brilliant effect. A grand cathedral is to be erected by order of the Czar in every city in the empire in commemoration of the assassination of Alexander II. The poor peasants are just able to keep soul and body together, and the cattle plague is taking off thousands of their cattle, yet these costly cathedrals are built by order of the Czar, who holds the key to the treasury of the empire.

There are said to be four thousand bells in the city, and when they are all sounded, as on Easter morning, the effect is enchanting, as the great bell of the cathedral, which takes a dozen men to toll it and is said to sound like the rolling of distant thunder.

Some one, in his travels, describes the ringing of all the bells in Moscow on Easter eve: "At midnight the great bell of the cathedral tolled. Its vibrations seemed to be the rolling of distant thunder, and they were instantly accompanied by the noise of all the small bells in Moscow. Every inhabitant was stirring, and the rattling of carriages in the street was greater than at noon-day. The whole city was in a blaze, lights were seen in all the windows, and innumerable torches in the streets. The tower of the cathedral was illuminated from its foundation to its cross. The same ceremony takes place in all the churches, and what is truly surprising, considering their number, they are all equally crowded. We hastened to the cathedral, it was filled with a prodigious assembly, consisting of all ranks of both sexes, bearing lighted wax tapers, to be afterward heaped as vows upon the different shrines. The walls of the ceilings, and every part of the building, are covered with the pictures of saints and martyrs. In the moment of our arrival, the doors were shut, and on the outside appeared Plato, the archbishop, preceeded by banners and torches, and followed by all his train of priests, with crucifixes and censors, who were making three times, in procession, the tour of the cathedral, chanting with loud voices and glittering in sumptuous vestments bespangled with gold, silver and precious stones. The snow has not melted so rapidly in the cathedral within the Kremlin as in the streets of the city. This magnificent procession was constrained, therefore, to move upon planks over the deep mud which surrounded the cathedral. After completing the third circuit, they all halted opposite the great doors, which were all closed. The archbishop, with a censor, then scattered incense against the doors and over the priests.

Suddenly, these doors were opened, and the effect was magnificent beyond description. The immense throng of spectators within, bearing innumerable tapers, formed two lines, through which the archbishop entered, advancing with his train to a throne near the center. The profusion of lights, in all parts of the cathedral, and among others of the enormous chandeliers in the center, the richness of the dresses, and the vastness of the assembly, filled us with astonishment."

XI.

THE PALACE, WITH ITS TREASURES.   THE LOASE
MARKET.   THE FOUNDLING HOSPITAL.

OUR visit to the palace was an interesting one, as we pass through the different halls, especially the Hall of St. George, founded by Catherine II., and dedicated to the order of St. George. The coat of arms of Russia is an effigy of St. George on a white horse. All these great halls are full of interesting historical relics and paintings. The crowns worn by the Emperors and Empresses are numerous and costly, especially the one made by order of Peter the Great for Catherine I., with its two thousand five hundred diamonds, besides other precious jewels. Among the valuable paintings is one of immense size, of Alexander I., entering Paris with his army, in 1813. 'Near this is a fine marble statue of Napoleon, which causes to rush through the mind the wonderful events connected with the latter's march to Moscow, in 1812, and the almost entire destruction of his army of fifty

A HALT ON THE HIGHWAY.

thousand, and the next year the march of the Russians triumphantly into Paris. Among the old carriages, which are heavy, and quaint enough, is one presented by Queen Elizabeth, in 1580, to Czar Boris Godunof, whom she wanted to marry. We were shown the coronation chairs and robes, and canopy, (the latter made of real gold cloth), of the present Emperor and Empress, and many others. Our guide informs us that at the coronation there were over a million of people present, and the utmost good order prevailed, and that it is said to have cost the government at least twenty million dollars.

On account of the failure of the crops and the cattle disease in Russia, a great many peasants flock to Moscow, and we visited the *Tolkatschta*, or *Loase* market, so called from the great number of poor, dirty people, who gather in a large square, where old clothes, old shoes, and the poorest of cast-off garments, furniture, cooking utensils, etc., are sold, and where a dinner of dirty soup is furnished for two cents. We were told to divest ourselves of our watches, and everything of value, for a more God-forsaken crowd could not be found. We were glad to escape with our thumb and finger upon our nose, and brush and shake ourselves well. It has become such a nuisance that the papers of Moscow are calling the attention of the city authorities to the effect it is having upon the sanitary condition of the city. Our guide was an intelligent Russian, who had lived in Buffalo, N. Y., and was a citizen of the United States. He showed me his passport, which has to be renewed every year, but the government has become so alarmed that they are about to compel all residents to become citizens of Russia or leave the country. The censorship of the press is very severe. All foreign papers are closely examined, and if any article appears reflecting upon Russia, the papers are suppressed, or a block of ink is stamped upon the offensive sentence. In one of the papers which I got, a part of an article on Russia was stamped in black, obliterating every letter.

The inconvenience of having a press censorship is illustrated by some recent incidents in Russia. A newspaper, published in the Caucasus, has been compelled to suspend, because its particular censor chose to move to a distant town, and to insist that proof sheets be sent him daily for his inspection, a condition incompatible with the prompt publication of the paper. One of these lord censors in St. Petersburg compelled a compiler of a small book on French literature to correct the clause, "*La majeste de ma nature*," on the ground that the word majesty should only be applied to the Czar.

Russia has two great foundling hospitals, one at St. Petersburg and one in Moscow, probably the largest and most complete in the world. This hospital admits yearly about fifteen thousand children, and they are not left, as in the hospital which we visited in St. Petersburg, at the door, or handed to the nurse through the window, but taken to a room set apart for that purpose. No questions are asked but "Has the child been baptized?" and if so, "By what name?" The child is then registered in the books of the institution, a number is assigned to it, which is worn around its neck, and figures on its cot, while a receipt, showing the same number, is given to the bearer of the child, in order to enable her to visit, or even to claim it, at any future period, up to the age of ten years. The child is then handed to its future foster parent, who happens to be first on the list among the uumber who are waiting in attendance. These women often deposit their own children at the hospital a few hours previous. They get about ten or twelve cents a day as nurses. After remaining in the institution four weeks, and having been vaccinated, they are sent with their nurses to the villages, where the latter belong. About fifty per cent of the children die in one year, owing to the severe climate and owing to the universal custom among the Russian peasantry of leaving young infants alone, for several hours at a time, with the "soska," or kind of milk poultice at their mouths, to munch, which often chokes them. Russia is not behind any other nation in the world in her hospitals. The Grand Duchess of Russia, widow of George of Mecklenburg-Strelitz, maintains a dozen large hospitals in various towns, and is engaged in many public benevolent institutions, and has lately established a new private eating-house for students in St. Petersburg. She is the wealthiest woman in the world, and inherited her wealth from Catherine II.

XII.

THE PETROFSKI PALACE AT MOSCOW. THE JOURNEY TO NIJNI-NOVGOROD. THE PANORAMA OF THE OKA AND THE VOLGA. A GALA DAY.

WE rode out to a Russian encampment, near the Petrofski palace and park built by Catherine II. Napoleon retired to this place after the Kremlin became untenable. There were said to be sixty thousand soldiers in camp. When the officer of the day learned that we were Americans, he was exceedingly attentive to us, and took us through the encampment to the officers' quarters, kitchen, and to witness the drill. The soldiers were stout and robust, but did not look intelligent, and the animal seemed to preponderate. They receive only two copecks, or one cent a day for their services. Every able-bodied man in Russia, who has attained his twenty-first year, is obliged to serve in the army, and no substitutes are allowed. The regular period of service is fifteen years, six of which are spent in active service, and nine in the reserve. Russia has more than a million of men under arms.

Our journey from Moscow to Nijni-Novgorod, an ancient city founded in 1222, was interesting as giving us an opportunity to see the peasants and their villages, and this Asiatic town, with its motley crowd of Persians, Armenians, Tartars and Caucasians. We first take a carriage and drive about the city, and on our way across the bridge over the Volga we meet a large number of Asiatics, some on foot and some in vehicles, with their goods and camping stuff. A steamer has just arrived on the Volga from the Caspian Sea, and one thousand five hundred miles via Orenburg, at the lower end of the Ural Mountains and Central Asia. We get a splendid view of the city from Muzavief's tower, and a grand panorama of the Volga and Oka Rivers, with the forests of masts down the river as far as the eye can reach. The city is below us on both sides of the Volga, and although it has but fifty thousand inhabitants at this time, when the great annual fair is in operation it appears much larger, as the great number of shops and bazars extend over considerable space between the Volga and Oka Rivers. A short distance from the tower is "Othos," a terrace built by Emperor Nicholas, where there is a beautiful park, with flowers and seats, from which we get a distant view of the cultivated fields over which the Volga overflows in the spring, making the plains rich with fertile deposits. The Volga is covered with steamers and barges, and we are interested in the large number of Tartars, as they are engaged in unloading the products of different kinds for the fair. A large monument was erected here by the Emperor, dedicated to a patriotic butcher, "Minin," who raised money to equip an army to drive away the Tartars who held possession of the city. We return to the fair, which was said to have been held here as long ago as the fourteenth century, and is visited sometimes by two hundred thousand to three hundred thousand persons, mostly Asiatics, and from eighty million to one hundred million dollars changes hands during the six weeks or two months the fair lasts. The ancient form of trade is still kept up, but will be superseded by railroads and the establishment of banks, etc. Dealers are obliged to offer their goods here at regular times of holding the fair. The iron and other metals stored in the miles of buildings have been brought here from the Ural Mountains and Siberia, at a great cost, for sale and distribution, within a few miles of their place of production. Dealers are obliged to buy large stocks, and get a credit of one or two years. This adds largely to the price, and in these times of small margins and great competition the more modern way of short time or cash sales must be resorted to, and the fair will be done away with, or change its peculiarity. Railroads already extend to the Ural Mountains. We were interested in examining the bazar, which contains such a variety of stones and minerals from Siberia, and silver made into different fancy articles from the Caucasian Mountains. Turks were here with their goods, and Tartars, and everything had an oriental appearance—silks and rugs from Persia. The articles made from malacite and lapis-lazuli, and other stones from Siberia, were numerous and beautiful, and a day spent in this bazar was full of intense interest, on account of the novel people and their productions, which one continually meets. The tea that one gets here is said to be superior, on account of its coming from China overland, for it is claimed that all tea, notwithstanding all precaution, is deteriorated by crossing the ocean. The tea is all served with lemon, in glass tumblers; a silver spoon is always in the glass, which is said to prevent the hot tea breaking the tumbler.

It was a gala day at Nijni-Novgorod to-day, as Grand Duke Nicholas, brother of the Emperor, had a grand reception here, and the flags were flying, and everything presented a gay appearance. He was here with his son and other officers of the army, under the charge of the Governor and chief of police. Five or six carriages in all would drive rapidly through the streets, and visit some of the large bazars of the fair, and away the masses would rush to get sight of him, and all day long the people were running after him, whichever way he would go. After dining with the Governor (whose house is in the center of the fair, and the lower part occupied by a bazar for the sale of curious articles from Bokhara and other parts of Central Asia), he had a reception on the streets by two companies of Cossacks in their peculiar uniform, with spears or harpoons. The Cossacks may be very brave and dangerous, but they did not present a very attractive military appearance.

Before leaving on the train I took a stroll down by the wharves, which are ten or twelve miles long, and all along I stop to look at the Tartars unloading and loading the curious-looking craft with grain, hides, wooden boxes, wine, skins from the Caucasus, madder and cotton from Bokhara, and almost every description of merchandise peculiar to the East, and loading European goods. It was seven o'clock in the evening, and all were leaving their work to go to their suppers, and as they passed me, men and women, I never saw a more dirty, savage-looking set, and, being alone, I did not feel safe, and hurried to the station, meeting our guide looking for me, who had become alarmed at my absence, and some of the party did not quiet the ladies by their stories of people who had been knocked down and stripped by the Tartars on the outskirts of the city only a day or two before.

A great many gypsies who wander over the Eastern world were at the fair, and the singing of some of the young women in the restaurants was entertaining, and showed considerable harmony and good voices. The outskirts of the fair are more interesting than the center for observation and study. The constant succession of carts in long strings, the crowds of laborers, the knots of earnest-looking traders with long beards, the itinerant venders of liquid refreshments and white rabbit skins, the greasy, slovenly-looking monks collecting the copecks of those who fear to withhold their charity lest their transactions be influenced by the evil one, the frequent beggars, pleading for the most part that they have been burned out and showing the most dreadful-looking sores as evidence of their veracity—all these men and things attest the present importance of the fair of Nijni. The sales and purchases represent sixteen million sterling, which pass through the hands of one hundred and fifty thousand to two hundred thousand traders. The bakers are bound to make daily returns of the quantity of bread which they sell, and it is in this manner that a rough estimate of the daily population is made. Great quantities of dried fish are sold at Nijni. The annual value of the sturgeon alone taken in the Volga is estimated at two million five hundred thousand rubles. Fairs were held here as early as 1366, and tradition points to a still earlier origin. Great caravans are started from China, overland, which are six months to a year reaching Nijni-Novgorod.

XIII.

RETURN TO MOSCOW. THE HUTS AND VILLAGES. PEASANT LIFE.

WE noticed on our return to Moscow the Russian villages with their huts made of logs and thatched roofs, out on the hot plains without a tree to shelter the people from the burning sun. Not a farm house is to be seen anywhere, but all huddled together — men, women, children, dogs, pigs and cattle. You cannot tell the huts of the human from the beast's. The peasants wear sheepskin clothes and shoes made of some kind of bark, and the women red cotton frocks, with scarlet or some bright colored handkerchief on their heads when they are in church, and look gay enough. There does not seem to be much encouragement for a peasant to be industrious and try to get ahead in the world, as the land belongs to the whole village and is all cultivated together on the communal system, and the village is responsible for the entire sum, which the commune has to pay annually into the imperial treasury. Each of these communes keeps a list of the male peasants for the purpose of direct taxation. The government pays no attention to the number of persons who may be born between the times of the various revisions till the new revision takes place. (Gogol, in his "Dead Souls," uses this fact as the groundwork of his work.) Every peasant who pays these taxes is supposed to have a share of the communal land, and the amount of tax imposed has nothing to do with the quality or quantity of the land, but is entirely personal. The commune has to pay into the imperial treasury a fixed yearly sum, according to the number of its revision souls, and distributes the land among its members as it thinks fit. The revision of the land takes place about every fifteen years, and the land is then distributed according to the number of persons which the family contains. This would naturally occur after each census. But the various changes brought about in each commune by the deaths, the births, and the migrations, compel the villages to make the redistribution more frequently. In some districts they divide their lands yearly, while others do not do so till the lapse of two or more years. The richest and best cultivated communes make redistribution of their lands less frequently than poorer ones. When the territory is vast, as in the northern provinces, the land is common to many villages and constitutes a "ro-lost." Thus in the district of Olonetz, about six hundred villages are grouped in thirty communes. It is singular that even the German colonists on the banks of the Volga, although they received their lands in severalty, have united them under the communal system. There may arise a difficulty, because the active members of the various families would not be the same, and accordingly in some communes an attempt has been made to distribute the land according to the working powers of the families; but the allotment depends upon the will of the particular commune. The authority of the particular communal parliament is final and supreme. No peasant challenges it, and the government never interferes. The village parliament is presided over by the village elder, whose house is marked out conspicuously among the others, and who wears as a badge of office a small medal suspended from the neck by a thin brass chain. The decisions of the communal parliament are generally made by acclamation, but whenever an ambiguity arises, it is settled in the Western fashion—by a division. The attempt to introduce voting by ballot into these assemblies by the government, about fifty years ago, resulted in a failure. The cottages (izba) of Russian peasants are built of wood, the beams being laid crosswise and the roof jutting out far beyond the bases. The furniture is of a scanty description, and in addition to the chairs and tables there is a large "peck" or stove, upon which the family sleep, and the sacred "ikon" in the corner of the room, with a lamp burning before it, and every one who enters is expected to cross himself and bow before it; if this is not done it is considered a great mark of disrespect. The distribution of the meadow land takes place annually. The division of this and the arable land is performed by the peasants themselves, who invariably effect it with great accuracy. The minor rules with regard to the time and manner of cultivation of the land are all made subservient to the general advantage of the commune. For some of the above facts I am indebted to Mr. Mackenzie Wallace's work. It does not seem as if there would be any change from the communal system, as the law, since the serfs were emancipated, allows the commune to be broken up into severalty, but very few villages avail themselves of this permission. The system seems well adapted to the nature and habits of the Russian peasants, who are extremely ignorant, drunken and filthy, and only one in ten can read and write.

The condition of the Russian peasant during the days of serfdom must have been a terrible one, judging from some accounts we get from various sources—not unlike the condition of slaves in this country. We are told of one lady who had been a great beauty in her day, and being unwilling that the world should become too much informed about the decay of her charms, constituted one of her serfs her perruquier (wig maker), and the unhappy man was kept in captivity, never being allowed to quit a certain room. He, however, at length succeeded in making his escape, and the whole story became known. We read of women murdering their serfs, and one that was sentenced by the Empress Catherine to spend her life in a dungeon for her cruelties. Details are given of the terrible cruelties practiced by the nobles upon the serfs.

Serfdom was established in Russia by Boris

RUSSIAN PEASANT.

Godunof, who issued a decree about the year 1600, forbidding peasants to leave the lands on which that date should find them. Earlier traces of it are found in the middle of the thirteenth century, during the Tartar dominion. The inhabitants of towns and villages were then forbidden to leave them without permission ; but the full and final attachment of the soil was not consummated until the close of the sixteenth century. Turgenief had a horror of serfdom, and left Russia to study in Germany. He writes: "That life, that society, that sphere—if such an expression may be used—to which I belonged, the sphere of serf-holding landowners, contained nothing to hold me to my country. On the contrary, almost everything that I saw around me aroused within me a sense of annoyance, contempt and dissatisfaction. I could not breathe the same air, I could not remain in the same environment with that which I abhorred. It was necessary for me to withdraw at a distance from my enemy, in order to charge the more forcibly against him from a distance. In my eyes that enemy had a defined name—it was the right of serf-holding. Under this inscription I collected and concentrated all that against which I resolved to fight to the last, with which I swore never to reconcile myself. This was my 'Hannibal oath.'" Turgenief regarded the serf as "a strong and useful laborer, endowed with an instinctive sense of morality, but being isolated from the world, and unable to speak a word in his own behalf." The classes of nobility, on the other hand, he considered as "useless consumers of the peasant's labor, to which they were entitled by the chance of birth ; as demoralized by affluence and laziness, as demoralizing all that came into contact with them."

XIV.

NIHILISM AND ITS POSSIBILITIES. TURGENIEF, THE NOVELIST.

PROFESSOR MORFILL writes: "Turgenief, the greatest of Russian novelists, in his powerfully written works, giving harrowing descriptions of the miserable condition of the Russian serfs, in his series of sketches called 'Memoirs of a Sportsman,' and a succession of able works reviewing all classes of Russian society, invented the word Nihilist."

I have never read a more pathetic story than "The Gentleman's Retreat," and as some one says, "there are touches in it worthy of George Eliot." The great novelist died in Paris while we were in Russia, a great loss to Russia and to the world. He accomplished for the emancipation of the serfs what Harriet Beecher Stowe did for the emancipation of five million slaves in our own country, and in his "Fathers and Children," and "Smoke," Turgenief has grappled with the nihilistic ideas, which have for a long time been so current in Russia. The spread of Nihilism so rapidly in Russia was caused, no doubt, by the emancipation of twenty-two million of the serfs, in 1861, by Alexander II., who liberated more human beings by his own power and free will than any other person. The nobles have hated the Czars ever since, for they hired out a vast number of the serfs, who were a great source of income to them, and this emancipation act deprived them of great sources of revenue. The peasants and lower class of people were very much attached to their great liberator, and they never tire of looking at his uniform and sword, with the spots of blood upon them, which he wore when assassinated, which are exposed in a glass case in one of the churches in St. Petersburg. They would almost tear any one in pieces who should say anything against the Czar. Nihilism, no doubt, is largely confined to the nobility, and to the students in the eight or ten colleges, who begin to understand that their liberties are taken from them by the autocrat of all the Russians, and that Russia is not advancing like the other nations of the world, and are becoming uneasy and dissatisfied, and therefore the frequent outbreaks among this class. In order to discuss properly the modern revolutionary movement in Russia, we must go back to Alexander Herzen, whom, however, it would be somewhat unfair to class among Nihilists, as he was a man of much more temperate character. Herzen was born in Moscow, in 1812, the son of a Russian nobleman. He early developed a taste for socialistic theories, and was a great student of the writings of Hegel. Having inherited a large property from his father, he resolved to quit Russia, invested his money in foreign securities, and took up his permanent residence in the west of Europe. In some most interesting papers, published in the *Polar Star*, in Russia, under the title of "The Past and My Thoughts," he has given rigorous sketches of the strange life which he led in intimate friendship with the leading political exiles, among others Kossuth and Orsini. He founded in London a Russian paper of democratic principles, called the *Kolokol* (*The Bell*). In a supplement, entitled "Under Judgment," minute details were given of cases of injustice and oppression on the part of the Government. These were ordinarily so accurate that it is impossible to doubt they must have been communicated by persons of high official position in Russia. It also circulated, to a great extent, in the country, but, of course, secretly. In spite of its democratic tone, it was always distinctly patriotic and Russian. In 1865 Herzen removed to Switzerland, and died in 1870. He was the author of a great many works, besides conducting his journal, among them several novels, and any one reading them would conclude that Herzen was an honest man and a true patriot. Of a very different type was Michael Bakounin, who may be said in some sort to have been the founder of nihilism. He was born in 1814, of a wealthy Russian family, and early showed signs of insubordination. Thus having been gazetted in the Imperial Russian Guards, at the age of twenty-two, he was forced to leave the military service. At Moscow he joined a club of intelligent men, who were great students of the philosophy of Hegel. Among these were Herzen, Granovski, professor of history at the University of Moscow, and author of some valuable works, and Belinski, the genial critic, and other prominent scholars. In the year 1841 Bakounin went to Berlin, that he might study the doctrines of Hegel more thoroughly; afterward he removed to Paris, and having refused to return at the command of the Russian Government, was now an exile. He afterward mixed himself up with the affairs of the revolution at Dresden, was arrested, and sentenced to death. This sentence was, however, commuted to imprisonment for life. In 1851 he was surrendered to the Russian Government, and was imprisoned in the fortress of Petropovloski in St. Petersburg. His punishment was afterward mitigated by banishment to Siberia; he succeeded in making his escape in an American ship to Japan, and arrived in London in 1861. On his arrival in London he joined Herzen, and became one of his co-laborers on the *Kolokol*, to which he communicated a much more rabid tone. In 1865 the office of the *Kolokol* was removed to Geneva, and here Bakounin plunged into the wildest socialism. He died in 1878, having been unceasing in his efforts to propagate nihilism. One of his agents, Nechaer, had deluged Russia with political pamphlets of extreme views. Nechaer's trial brought to light the fact that Bakounin had filled Russia—especially influencing young persons—with political papers of the wildest and most rabid kind; he praised Karokasor, who attempted the Czar's life in 1866, but deprecated further efforts at assassination, as the Czar must be reserved for the judicial sentence of the people ; the aim of the revolution was to be universal destruction ; "absolute void must be created, for if one old social form were left, it would be an embryo out of which all the other forms would renew themselves."

XV.

THE SOCIALISTIC PRESS. THE ORGAN OF THE INSTITUTION. TOLSTOI AND THE SUPERIOR COUNCIL. THE END.

I THINK there is now a Russian socialistic press in Geneva, which is very active. Many articles appear in the Little Russian language, especially in a magazine entitled "*Gromasln.*" The Nihilists are extremely active, and we can hardly take up a daily paper but we read accounts of assassinations and murders. The policy of the government appears to be to suppress, as much as possible, the doings of the Nihilists. Many are sent off to Siberia, without trial, or without it being known. It would seem that they are a misguided, desperate class of men, and that nothing can be accomplished by such unwise measures as assasssination, but to unsettle the affairs of Russia and cause an immense expense by keeping so large a number engaged in protecting the country from their dastardly deeds. No person is allowed to go in or out of Russia without a passport, and every newspaper is examined, and on every article that criticises the government, or says anything about Nihilism, a block of ink is stamped across the objectionable words. All of this espionage must keep an immense number of officials employed, and it would seem that financial ruin would come upon the country in time, on account of the enormous expenses. During the last ten years no less than one hundred and sixty-five thousand prisoners have been transported to Siberia, many of them without any trial, by simple order or resolution of the commune, never having even seen a judge, on suspicion, perhaps, of being Nihilists. Twenty years ago the exiles traversed on foot all the distance between Moscow and the place to which they were dispatched; now they go part of the way on foot, in wagons, and on special barges, or floating prisons, which are overcrowded, and are usually kept in such filthiness that disease is created. Diptheria and typhus fever kill adults and children, especially the latter. Corpses of children are thrown out at nearly every station. When the season and state of the river permits, parties of five hundred convicts, each with women and children, leave the Tomsk prison every week, and begin their foot journey to Irkutsk and Tranchaitalin. The suffering is terrible, and their number is increasing every year.

The Czar convened the Superior Council on the 10th of March for the purpose of considering the social question. They considered the question whether there really exists a powerful Nihilist party, and if so, what their wants, and how to satisfy or crush them, as the demands of the country may require. The council was composed of representatives of the ruling classes, including Count Tolstoi, minister of the interior, Lieutenant-General Tchernaieff, General Ignatieff and Miljutine, M. Abassa, and all the heads of the administrative departments.

APPENDIX.

I.

THE PEASANTS OF RUSSIA.

The peasants of Russia are a superstitious class from the cradle to the grave. Charms, incantations and mystic remedies in the case of disease are common. A feast is held in Russia on the occasion of a death, but also on many other stated days the dead and ancestors of the village are commemorated. Even the nobles used to have a noise made outside the house to keep the evil spirits off. Up to this day the old women cross themselves in orthodox fashion on the railway trains as soon as the cars start. The nobility of Russia have been so brought under the western European influences that one can not see in them the anomalous characteristics of the Scythians or Slavonians, as among the peasantry. They are a contented, docile, sturdy race, and, as were the race from which they descended, are brave, as has been proved on many a battlefield. Sir Henry Havelock bears testimony to the virtues and bravery of the Russian soldier. No country can show greater heroism than they exhibited amid the horrors of Shipka pass. With all their heroism they are servile and terribly given to drunkenness. Probably they are the most drunken people in the world. The ordinary beverage is a kind of fermented barley (kvas), somewhat sour, but by no means disagreeable to the palate, and a coarse kind of corn brandy called "vocka."

According to an old work, "It is a custom over all Muscovie that a maid in time of wooing sends to that suitor whom she chooseth for her husband, such a whip curiously wrought by herself, in token of her subjection unto him." Another Russian writer also tells us that it was usual for the husband on the wedding day to give his bride a gentle stroke over the shoulders with his whip, to show his power over her. In some story it is related that a wife complained to her husband that he did not love her; but upon his expressing surprise at the doubt, she gave as a reason that he had never beaten her! The bridegroom knew nothing of his bride. She was only allowed to be seen a few times before marriage by his female relatives, and on these occasions all kinds of tricks were played. A stool was placed under her feet that she might seem taller, or a handsome female attendant or a better looking sister were substituted. "Nowhere," says one writer, "is there such trickery practiced with reference to brides as at Moscow."

A Nihilist in Moscow told me that he had given up trying to accomplish anything by assassination; indeed, he did not see how any change could be brought about so long as all the peasants are contented with their lot and never desire to better their condition by leaving Russia for America or any other country. I do not remember ever to have seen but one Russian who had become an inhabitant of this country.

Russia seems to be taking pride in her own language and literature, and instead of imitating the French, they are developing a vigorous individuality, and has a brilliant prospect for her language, and is fast absorbing the Finish dialect, the Polish and Lithunian.

II.

MARRIAGE IN RUSSIA.

The Russian merchant, the citizen of Odessa, retains to this day some of the ancient customs of his fore-fathers. The primitive character of Russian nationality has to battle hard against the influence of European civilization. Family influence, and especially that of the home circle, however, still exists in full force. Father and mother have complete moral authority over their children of both sexes, no matter how old the latter may be. This authority shows itself principally in the words and actions of the father. He conducts his household as he pleases, and among the trading class it is very rare indeed to hear of a son or daughter acting in opposition to a father's will. In general the father is feared and respected, the mother respected and loved. Nowhere is home life —the intimate family life—so fully developed as in Russia, and that more particularly in the class which is here called merchant citizen.

The father, therefore, decides the marriage of his children, and what he requires before all else is that the future wife or husband should belong to the orthodox Greek Church and have a good reputation. Young men may marry at eighteen, young girls at sixteen. Whether the future pair know each other or not, there is always a match-maker engaged to make the overtures and to carry on the negotiations on this delicate subject. "Popping the question" is a profession that requires a great deal of art and intelligence in the person who exercises it. In the first place a match-maker must be a widow, not younger than thirty-five years, and not older than fifty. She must be lively, good looking and full of fun and wit. It is quite indispensable that she should have the "gift of gab," that, as the Russian proverb has it, she need not feel for her words in her pocket. A match-maker ought to know everything, without showing it. Very often the match-maker is the widow of a priest. After the death of her husband, when she sets up in her profession, she is sure to have a large number of customers, both rich and influential, to help her on in any difficulties, particularly if her husband, during his lifetime, had acquired the love and respect of his parishioners in the exercise of his ministry. St. Petersburg, or any other large Russian city, seldom either hates or despises the priest. The "white" or secular clergy are, generally speaking, well instructed and well read, and lead a sober and laborious life, devoting their whole time to the duties imposed upon them by the church. Constantly under the eyes of the Holy Synod of the Emperor himself and of the whole of Europe, even if they do not possess all the qualities necessary to constitute them good ministers, they take care to be outwardly all that they should be.

THE MATCH-MAKER.

The match-maker is the intimate friend of all parents who have children to marry and of young lovers of both sexes. She is always on the outlook, and knows how to guess the inclination of her customers and the best time to commence operations. The custom is that neither the parents nor the young people should show that the latter desire to contract a marriage; in fact, they pretend entire ignorance on the subject. "Well, Ivan Ivanitch," says the matchmaker to the father, "you have the goods and I have the buyer; do you not think it is time to find a place for Machinka? Come St. Alexander's Day (the holy man) she will have attained her tenth year, with six added to her. What say you?" "Why, I don't say no if my daughter says yes. Speak to her. It is her business, not mine. I am an old man now, and have forgotten all about these sorts of things." Now, the match-maker knows very well that Machinka is in love with the young Andevrimkoff, her uncle's clerk. "Come, Ivan Ivanitch, the thing is very well as it is; Machinka won't say no, you'll see." "Very well," says the old man, "tell me who is the predestined engaged one? Who is he? the brave fellow, and where is he?" "Guess," says she. The old man names all the young men he knows without ever mentioning the right one, although he is perfectly aware all the time who he is; but such is the usage. At last the match-maker names him and adds: "Marriages are made in heaven, you know."

When all this is settled they send for the mother, and the same scene is repeated, with this difference—that she bursts into tears when she gives her consent. And now takes place the third scene of the first act. The young lady is sent for. The match-maker begins by making a long speech, in which she describes the happiness of the marriage state, particularly the quiet happiness of the young lady's own parents; speaks of the blessings of God that had evidently been bestowed upon them in the gift of children. She then continues to tell of the pleasures of becoming a mother, of parental love and of the way in which the young lady's parents had brought up their daughter, and concludes by a serious exhortation to respect and obey her parents. All this time Machinka is standing before the tribunal, listening with downcast eyes and blushing cheeks. The foregoing scenes are then acted over again, and Machinka does not succeed any more than her parents in finding out the young gentleman's name. At last the match-maker declares it. If he is accepted by the young lady she throws herself at her parents feet and declares she never wishes to leave them, but that, if it is her destiny, she is willing to desire their blessing.

The father then sends for the members of his household, even to the janitor of the building; all sit down and remain perfectly still for a moment; they then rise, say a prayer mentally, making the sign of the cross, and the father declares to all present that his daughter is asked in marriage; that she has accepted the offer because she believes it to be her destiny and the will of God; finally he gives her his blessing. All then congratulate the parents of the young lady. Everybody sheds tears at the thought of the separation and bowing leave the room.

The family now remain alone with the match-maker to treat of the marriage outfit; the parents ask what the young man has, although they know very well; but it is the custom. Then the match-maker begins: "Well, Ivan Ivanitch, you give the principal bundle of goods, but what do you give into the bargain?" "Hum!" says the old man, "the goods I furnish are so good that I consider anything else useless. Let us first know what the future husband has." The match-maker then mentions, one after the other, everything the gentleman is to bring towards housekeeping. The father listens and enumerates all he is to give his daughter, and begins thus: "A large double bed, complete." The match-maker says; "It is the custom;" the young lady blushes, the mother sighs. The father continues: "Two marten sable cloaks, one of fox fur, fifteen Lyons silk and satin dresses, ten real Paris bonnets, twelve pairs of shoes, three chemises, one nightgown and one petticoat," etc. After many observations on both sides, everything is concluded. The day is appointed for the young couple to be presented to each other. They then separate. The next day the bride's family go to church to give thanks for the marriage in prospect, which they must now make known to their friends and relations.

THE FIRST KISS.

When the bridegroom is presented the whole house is in confusion. All the relations, friends and neighbors on both sides are invited to the house of the bride. When all the expected company are assembled the match-maker comes in, leading the bridegroom by the hand, and going straight to the head of the house, presents him. The father first, then the mother, kisses him. The bride's father then leads the young man to a table covered with a white cloth. On the table is a silver salver, with a loaf of bread on it, and on the bread a salt-cellar, with salt. Two rings—one of gold, the other of silver—are placed on a small silver tray before a golden image of the Virgin Mary, holding the Child Jesus in her arms. With this image they bless the future couple. All the company stand, the mother holding the bride, completely dressed in white, by the hand, surrounded by all her dearest friends and companions. All bow before the image. The father takes the image, the mother the bread and salt ; the young couple then kneel under the image, and are first blessed by the father, the latter then takes the bread and salt from the hands of the mother and gives her the image, and the same ceremony is repeated. After this the father and mother of the bridegroom do the like. Then comes the giving of the rings ; the bride's father gives the golden ring to the bridegroom, the silver one to the bride. They are now affianced to each other, and give each other the first kiss. When the ceremony is over, the company enjoy themselves; they chat, laugh, eat and drink, and separate after having fixed the day for the marriage. During the interval between the ceremony and the marriage the bridegroom spends all his evenings with his bride, often tête-à-tête.

THE CEREMONY.

Then follows the marriage ceremony. It is also called the coronation, because, during the ceremony, a crown is placed on the heads of the affianced. Then the priest offers them a cup of wine, of which they both drink, as a sign of the union they have contracted. A solemn procession is led by the officiating priest, the bride and bridegroom following him round the desk placed in the center of the church, upon which is laid the Bible. This is meant to represent the joys which await them, the ties which they contract and the eternity of these ties. During the public celebration of the marriage the rings worn by the young people are exchanged, the husband now wearing the silver one, the bride the golden. From the church the company is invited to the house of the bridegroom's father. A week after they return to church, when the priest lifts the crown from their heads. This is the final consecration of marriage.

All the clergy that assisted at the blessing in the church expect to partake of the marriage feast. When rich merchants marry their children they spare nothing to make the ceremony splendid. Generally the carriage that takes them to the church is gilt, and drawn by four, sometimes six, horses—beautiful dappled grays. The marriage over, the bride is taken home to her new family. The coachman and the postillions are often richly dressed in azure velvet, with gold or gilt buttons; their belts and the ribbons streaming from their hats are all gold galoons. The reins of the horses, as well as their manes, are dotted with bunches of pink and blue ribbons; two huge men servants, with round hats, livery coats and knee-breeches, dazzling with blue and gold, are perched behind the carriage. This equipage hired for the occasion, costs not less than $200, but custom will have it so.

THE FEAST.

The banquet is ordered at some fashionable confectioner's. Nothing is wanting—silver, crystal, flowers and lusters laden with candles of the purest wax. The most perfect order reigns at these repasts. The finest wines flow in abundance, and music plays from time to time during the whole repast. The young married pair occupy seats about the middle of the table, the parents supporting them on both sides—the rest of the company take seats according to the degree of relationship or rank. If they want a very grand dinner, they order a "General's" dinner, which costs $30 more than an ordinary one. At this dinner, so ordered, the master of ceremonies invites a real old pensioned off General, who is received with all the reverence due to his rank, and seated in the place of honor. He is the first to drink the health of the young couple, and is always helped before any one else. He never speaks unless it is absolutely necessary. He is there only for show, and he does his best, in return for the $20 paid him for his presence, to eat and drink as much as he can. He is accosted, when helped to anything, arack or wine, as your Excellency. He never refuses a single dish of all the thirty or more served on such occasions.

These dinners are always served after the French fashion. As the last roast disappears from the table, the champagne corks fly, the glasses are filled to the brim, the music strikes up, and huzzahs resound from all parts. But here comes the bride's father, with glass in hand, going up to her bowing, and making a most woeful face, saying that his wine was so bitter that he could not drink it until she had sweetened it. After a great deal of pressing she rises and gives her husband a kiss; her father still pretends that his wine is bitter, and it remains so until she has given her husband three kisses; each kiss not only sweetens his wine, but is accompanied with roars of laughter and bursts of applause. After dinner comes the ball and "general's walk." They lead him through all the rooms once every half hour, everybody salutes him as he passes along and he graciously replies by an inclination of the head. At last, at 3 o'clock in the morning, all the young girls and those who dressed the bride take her away, to undress her and put her to rest; the men do the same by the husband. The next morning the house of the newly married couple is again filled with the crowds of the evening before. The young wife is seated in a drawing-room on a sofa with a splendid tea service before her. One after the other approaches, salutes her and asks: "Have you slept well, madam? Do you feel rested after the fatigues of the last night?" She then offers tea, coffee or chocolate, according to the taste of the visitor. She is throned for the first time in all splendor as the mistress of the house. The most intimate friends remain to spend the day with the young pair. A week after the marriage the wife's family gives a series of dinner parties, evening parties and balls. These fêtes sometimes last for a fortnight, or even three weeks or a month, and so the young people gradually subside into their ordinary every-day life.

III.

HOW THE RUSSIANS KEEP WARM.

The Russians have a great knack of making their winter pleasant. You feel nothing of the cold in those tightly built houses where all doors and windows are double, and where the rooms are kept warm by big stoves hidden in the walls. There is no damp in a Russian house, and the inmates may dress indoors in the lightest gards, which contrast oddly with the mass of furs and wraps they don when going out. A Russian can afford to run no risk of exposure when he leaves the house for a walk or drive. He covers his head and ears with a fur bonnet, his feet and legs with felt boots lined with wool or fur, which are drawn over the ordinary boots and trousers, and reach up to the knees ; he next cloaks himself in a top coat with a fur collar, lining and cuffs ; he buries his hands in a pair of fingerless gloves of seal or bear skin. Thus equipped, and with the collar of his coat raised all around so that it muffles him up to the eyes, the Russian exposes only his nose to the cold air ; and he takes care frequently to give that organ a little rub to keep the circulation going. A stranger who is apt to forget the precaution, would often get his nose frozen if it were not for the courtesy of the Russians, who will always warn him if they see his nose " whitening," and will, unbidden, help him to chafe it vigorously with snow. In Russian cities walking is just possible for men during the winter, but hardly so for ladies. The women of the lower order wear knee boots ; those of shopping class seldom venture out at all ; those of the aristocracy go out in sleighs. The sleighs are by no means pleasant vehicles for nervous people, for the Kalmuck coachmen drive them at such a terrific pace that they frequently capsize.

RUSSIAN FINANCES.

The Russian budget was never known to show a surplus. That of 1882, just made public, shows a deficit of nearly $4,000,000, which is, however, an improvement over former years. The expenditures for railroads during the year was about $12,000,000, incurred by the pushing of the system of Russia proper into the Russian possessions in Turkestan. Of the total expenditures of $355,580,000, the army and navy consumed $117,000,000, which, considering the vastness of the forces kept up, is lower than the cost of our own military and naval forces. The Russian revenue has fallen off in respect to the tax on alcoholic liquor, very largely owing to the decrease in consumption following the increase of the tax on liquors forty per cent. Usually the receipts from this source are about $120,000,000, and they have fallen off one-third. For many years the Russian police were employed forcing the people to spend their money in the brandy shops and get drunk, so that the government might be benefited by the revenue. Prince Dolgoroukoff relates that he had seen policemen dragging people by main force into the liquor shops to get them drunk. That is an original way of securing revenue for the Czar's government. The Russian finances were very much disordered by the war with Turkey, which cost $600,000,000 or $700,000,000, and was accompanied by vast issues of paper currency which depreciated rapidly. The public debt of Russia is believed to be about $2,000,000,000, and is not probable that it will be reduced, as Russia is not likely to abandon the old Petrine policy of possessing a Mediterranean littoral, which involves European war, and she is at a continual and increasing expence, strengthening her power and lines of communication from the Ural mountains to the Pacific ocean—an empire vast and full of resources, wich some day will overshadow Russia in Europe in importance.

DURATION OF LIFE IN RUSSIA.

The paucity of medical men in Russia, writes a correspondent, and the habits of the rural population combine to make the Russian death rate the highest in Europe. Excepting the two capitals, where there are many German physicians, there is no district in the empire sufficiently supplied with doctors. According to the latest returns, the average duration of life in Russia is only twenty-six years. The mortality among infants is frightful. More than sixty per cent die before they reach their fifth year. Nearly two million children perish every year. Of eight million boys, only three million seven hundred and seventy thousand attain the age of military service—that is to say, their twenty-fifth year; and of these at least one million are found, by reason of shortness of stature and weakness of body, unfit for military duty.

RAILROADS IN RUSSIA.

Many officials there are at every station dressed in uniforms. The railroads are owned by the government, and it seems as if every country would be ruined by the numerous officials. Railroads are extending all over Russia, and the Czar has extensive plans according to accounts on hand, with the Czar as its most enthusiastic promoter. The proposal is to build eleven thousand seven hundred miles of railroad in two trunk lines, one starting from Iekaterinenberg on the eastern slope of the Ural mountains and running through Siberia to Yakutak and Nikolajen, with a branch connecting with China and the region of the Amoor river; while the second line is to begin at Astrachan, connect with Persia, Herat in Afghanistan and India, and have a branch to Bokhara and by way of Kashgar to Central Asia. The idea is to employ the army in the construction of the roads in times of peace, and it is judged that the work will occupy twenty years. There is thus no need of immediate worry as to Russia's object in undertaking so stupendous a task, if it really seriously contemplates it. It defines its own purpose as the development of its agriculture and commerce by a net-work of railroads like that of the United States. The people who are continually foreseeing Russia's seizure of India from Great Britain are, however, already declaring that this project has a strategic significance ; that it is of a piece with the Mery country, and that the Pacific part of the scheme is but a blind to facilitate the construction of a railroad south which would permit the quick concentration of large bodies of troops upon Afghanistan, Persia and Asiatic-Turkey.

In 1882 Russia's expenditure for railroads was twelve millions of dollars, incurred by pushing the system of Russia proper into the Russian possessions in Turkestan.

WELCH, FRACKER COMPANY'S

Recent Publications.

From "IN WESTERN LEVANT."

THE MASTERPIECE OF THE BOOK-MAKER'S ART.

NOW READY

In Western Levant

BY

FRANCIS C. SESSIONS

President of the Ohio Archæological and Historical Society

With over Fifty Vignette Illustrations by
HENRY W. HALL

Printed on Warren coated paper, title page in colors, exquisitely bound, with parchment label title, gilt top, etc.

Author, artist, and designer have combined successfully to make this the most superb product of exclusively American talent that has yet been placed upon the market.

12mo. Cloth. $1.50, post-paid.

THE TERRACES OF FEZ AT SUNSET.

From "Into Morocco."

INTO MOROCCO.

FROM THE FRENCH OF

PIERRE LOTI.

ILLUSTRATED BY

Benjamin Constant and Aimé Morot.

12mo, Cloth, $1.25.

EXTRACTS FROM THE PRESS.

"The hit of the year!"—*State Journal.*

"Full of color, picturesqueness and charming description." *From column review in N. Y. Tribune.*

"A famous book."—*New Orleans Picayune.*

"Rising from the perusal of these sparkling pages, the reader feels as if under the lingering influence of some wild dream."—*From a three-column review in the Hartford Times.*

"A very clever and readable volume by one of the most unhackneyed, entertaining and imaginative of living writers."—*N. Y. Sun.*

"'Into Morocco' is vivid in rich word-coloring, and every page charms with its quaint attractiveness."—*San Francisco Post.*

"Loti's account of travel into the interior of that country by no means lessens the feeling of mystery, but rather enhances it. He seems to have pursued his researches in a sort of dream, and while observing closely and describing clearly all he saw and heard, yet conveys throughout his book that same atmosphere of unreality and delicious languor, and one lays the book down with a sigh at having completed its perusal, and with the brain filled with visions of white-robed veiled figures, tents, hot, sandy deserts, and long trains of silently moving camels. It is an enchanting book, and the picturesque illustrations add not a little to its charms.—*Milwaukee Sentinel.*

"Only those who are familiar with the deep poetic feeling and power of description of Pierre Loti, can obtain any conception of the character of this book without reading it. Readers who love the romantic, will be delighted with the book."—*Cleveland Leader.*

"Loti is, above all else, a literary colorist, and the pictures are wonderfully warm, sensuous and glowing."—*Chicago Times.*

"Mr. Loti has an artist's eye for the picturesque."—*Milwaukee Wisconsin.*

"Rich in quotable extracts, for on every page is a picture worth impressing on the memory for its beauty. It is vivid and inspiring.—*Chronicle, San Francisco.*

"A famous book, intensely interesting, beautifully illustrated."—*New Orleans Picayune.*

"Delightful reading."—*Toledo Blade.*

"Sure of welcome. It is a series of emotions deeply felt, exquisitely translated."—*Boston Transcript.*

"Full of charm; not an effect is lost. We wish we had space to quote at fuller length from this fascinating book."—*Boston Literary World.*

"One of the most fascinating books of travel that has appeared this year."—*The Writer, Boston.*

"A book of sunshine."—*Chicago Herald.*

From "THE BANK TRAGEDY."

The Delightful Tale of French Life and Manners

EXPIATION

By TH. BENTZON

ADMIRABLY TRANSLATED

12mo. 35 cents.

"Far ahead of its fellows in theme and general treatment."—*World Herald*, Omaha.

"Attractive, clear, smooth and free. The interest deepens."—*Times*, Chicago.

"A charming novel, and a welcome addition to the store of first-class works."—*Morning Chronicle.*

"A beautiful example of life displayed. The plot is interesting, and characters strongly drawn."—*Chicago Tribune.*

"An admirable story."—*Albany Argus.*

"Charming and graceful."—*Boston Literary World.*

"It will be found delightful'"—*Geyer's Stationer.*

A FLORENTINE CHURCH.

From "On the Wing Through Europe."

"ON THE WING THROUGH EUROPE, by F. C. Sessions, Esq., is a modest and well written account of what a less accurate man would not have seen, and a clearly given description of what a sensible and thoughtful pair of eyes did see in Europe. The exceedingly good taste, which is evident on every page, is added to full and complete mention of what one most wants to read about, and yet finds so little written about, as related to these topics. The binding is in harmony with the plan and execution of the whole volume."
—*Home Journal.*

"They are written with a remarkable grace, ease and clearness of style. His mind quickly seizes the salient points of interest and besides penetrates into regions not so often described by the ordinary traveler. It is a very interesting and instructive little book, and reveals the author as a man of vigorous intellect, keen observation, deep sympathy and excellent powers of description."—*Adams, Mass., Transcript.*

"While written modestly, simply and with no effort at vivid description, it does more to place the scenes, incidents and historic associations of a tour through the British Isles and on the continent of Europe before the reader intelligently, than any similar work we have ever seen. The engravings are fine, and two letters of Rev. Dr. Hutchins on famous English Divines, add greatly to the value of the book."—*Cincinnati Herald.*

"The letters are well written, and the descriptions of scenery, incidents, etc., are peculiarly interesting, showing that Mr. Sessions has been a careful observer. * * * The book is an exceedingly handsome one in printing and binding, and the elegant illustrations it contains add very much to its value and interest. We can cordially commend the work to our readers. It should have a very large and general circulation."—*Dispatch.*

ANN HATHAWAY'S COTTAGE.

From "On the Wing Through Europe."

"It is entirely unpretentious, and written in a lively and pleasing style. A breezy freshness and evident sincerity pervade its pages, and it is pleasant to learn what an unpretentious writer can make out of the old cities and time-honored buildings, the ancient rookeries and much-travelled thoroughfares of these older lands. The printed text shows good taste, and the illustrations add to its value."—*Christian at Work.*

"ON THE WING THROUGH EUROPE is the title of just such a journal of a flying tour of Europe, during the year of the Paris Exposition, as we might expect from almost any one of our clear-headed and sensible men of business writing for the entertainment of friends at home. Lively, concise, straightforward, touching lightly but intelligently upon a multiplicity of topics, without falling into sentimentality on the one hand, or lapsing into a too prosaic literalness on the other, it is an agreeable and unaffected record of impressions of travel. Its author's brief descriptions of phases of transatlantic life, manners, customs, and scenes, and of memorable places and buildings, are distinguished by the business man's faculty for close and sharp observation of men and things, and of arriving at rapid and generally just conclusions concerning them."—*Harper's Monthly.*

"The vast material upon which the traveler had to work is certainly attractively and instructively used in the narrow limits to which he confined his writing. Not the least attraction of the work is the series of twenty fine engravings, certainly the finest illustrations ever published in a work of this kind."—*Times*

"A series of very sprightly and readable letters to the *Ohio State Journal*, and we must say that they have lost nothing of their freshness and interest by reappearing in book form. We are reading it with great pleasure. The mechanical execution of the work—as shown in letter-press and engravings—is excellent—very creditable to the taste of the publishers."—*Springfield Republic.*

A ROMAN OX-CART.

From "On the Wing Through Europe."

From "IN WESTERN LEVANT,"

NOW READY.

BY WHOSE HAND?

A NOVEL

By EDITH SESSIONS TUPPER,
Author of "By a Hair's Breadth," etc.

MORE STIRRING, CLEVER AND VIGOROUS THAN EVEN HER
PREVIOUS SUCCESSFUL NOVELS.

12mo, Paper, 35 Cents.

ADVANCE NOTICES:

"Edith Sessions Tupper's latest novel, 'BY WHOSE HAND,' is a distinct advance on her previous work in firmness of touch and method of treatment of her subject. The skill in plotmaking which the author manifests in a marked degree, makes the novel a fascinating one for those who wish to peruse a work of fiction which will hold the attention to the last paragraph. As a novelist, Mrs. Tupper improves with each work."—*N. Y. Press.*

"An original romance. The sedate reader (if any such remain) will find the story somewhat emotional, but will acknowledge its animation."—*Brooklyn Times.*

"The authoress has an imagination which is always vivid, and sometimes picturesque."—*Kate Field's Washington.*

JUST PUBLISHED

A PORTRAIT IN CRIMSONS

A bright and entertaining Drama-novel.

BY

CHARLES EDWARD BARNS.

Delicately printed on antique laid, bound in parchment paper, etc. 12mo. 35 cents.

Will be widely read and enjoyed by all readers of this successful author.

From "AS 'TIS IN LIFE."

From "AS 'TIS IN LIFE."

A STERLING NOVEL

The Chicago Tribune Prize Story.

By a Hair's Breadth.

By Edith Sessions Tupper.

READ WHAT THE PRESS HAS TO SAY OF IT.

" Her undoubted talents are of such an order that she may reasonably expect to attain high rank among the fictionists of her time."—*Chicago Herald.*

" The authoress of this work is a bright and rising novelist."—*N. Y. Press.*

" The incidents are ingenious and well wrought together. This work opens a new field of enterprise to the gifted and versatile authoress."—*Jamestown Journal.*

" This effort in the line of romance shows her power. Her pen is her weapon. She has shown what she can do. Her coming story, ' By Whose Hand ? ' will be looked for with interest. . . . . It goes without saying that every advantage that the plot presents is taken. The detail work of the story is above criticism. ' From the introspective to the mystical is but a step.' This step has been taken by one of the brightest women this country has seen." — *Buffalo News.*

" ' By a Hair's Breadth' is ingenious, free from affectation, and told with a degree of freshness and originality."— *N. Y. Sun.*

" It is the reportorial capacity wonderfully developed in Robert Fleming, the immensely clever reporter, that works up the Paul Raymond murder. ' By a Hair's Breadth ' has merit, and Edith Sessions Tupper's hero knows by experience the advantages to be derived from the plentiful use of the blue lead pencil."—*N Y. Times.*

" One of the brightest little stories that has come to us in some time. A terse dramatic style combined with the ability of painting striking descriptions with a touch of the brush shows that Mrs. Tupper is an artist of no mean ability, and her future work will be awaited with interest. Heretofore her work has been confined to lyrical poetry, but the story field should know her soon again."—*Morning Journal.*

VENICE.

From "On the Wing Through Europe."

WELCH, FRACKER COMPANY'S
EDITIONS OF
The Works of Charles Edward Barns.

A VENETIAN STUDY IN BLACK AND WHITE:

A drama-novel of stirring incident, clever intrigue, with a plot of startling development, the scenes shifting from Gotham to the city of the Doges.

DIGBY: CHESS PROFESSOR:

A happy and unique drama-novel of New York life, the interest centering in an exciting game of chess.

A DISILLUSIONED OCCULTIST:

An East Indian episode, gathering interest from a home-bound student of Hindu occultisms, and the recital of his tragic history.

THIRTY-FIVE CENTS EACH, POST-PAID.

THE AMARANTH AND THE BERYL:

A volume of poetical works.

SOLITARIUS TO HIS DÆMON:

Thoughts and reflections of a thinker in search of new truths in nature and the heart of man.
12mo. Bond parchment-paper binding, exquisitely printed on antique laid paper, with engraved title-pages, etc.

FIFTY CENTS PER COPY.

NOW READY.

THE PITH OF A FEW ADVANCE

PRESS NOTICES:

"Barns' works appeal to the more thoughtful class of readers."—*Mercury*.

"These poems are the product of a deep dramatic instinct.... 'Solitarius to his Dæmon' is an excellent prose work."—*Telegram*.

"Mr. Barns' writings show the man of thought and culture... Solitarius is a work worthy of admiration. In this his talents show to advantage."—*Journal*.

"A work of high philosophy."—*Press*.

"They touch a responsive chord, and furnish food for many a fanciful reverie."—*News and Courier*.

"Vigorous, equally clever, and abounding in the results of much reading and thinking."—*Brooklyn Eagle*.

"Barns is a delightful essayist, and between his well-rounded periods is a rich mine of thought and philosophy, expressed in a most pleasing and impressive form. One of those books which is as pleasing in a second reading as in the first.....The poems are full of genius of the true point..... Our readers will find in these books a surprise and a delight."—*Christian at Work*.

"These drama-novels display much curious learning and a quaint humor."—*N. Y. Sun*.

"These works will prove a valuable addition to any library."—*San Francisco Call*.

From "IN WESTERN LEVANT."

"Barns has a fertile pen. His drama-novels are profuse in popular character, story and learning, written with marvellous fluency."....—*Brooklyn Eagle.*

"Barns is capable of excellent word-painting, admirable technique, and moreover, a noticeably sweet and tender versification....Many of the poems combine a vigorous and rich harmony with virility and manly sentiment."—*Philadelphia Transcript.*

"In spite of many defects, it is more than borne upon the reader that here are books with a genuine message for the world. The writer is humble, earnest and hopeful; not daunted by conventions, nor driven into mistaking them for truths, but yet respectful of them, acknowledging their place in the world. His reading has been wide, if not indeed profound, and has furnished him with a rich treasury of reference and allusion, and more than all, he is a sturdy promoter of manliness,—a virtue more than slightly underrated by many of his contemporaries....Barns will find many readers."—*Boston Herald.*

"Barns' books are unique, exciting, and beautiful specimens of their art."—*Phila. North American.*

"They cannot but be appreciated by all who seek real literary gems."—*San Francisco Chronicle.*

"A new writer has sprung into enviable prominence—a young poet, philosopher, and novelist, who has produced a series of volumes sufficiently original in thought and admirable in quality to merit the above titles......These writings have been remarkably amiably handled by the critics throughout the country, considering that they abound in crudities and literary faults; but they are the errors of a genius. Not a single page of his books but bears an individuality not to be mistaken....A sincere student of nature in all its phases. As Barns is young, and has had exceptional advantages as regards study and travel, there is no reason why, with his talents, he should not become an important factor in the literature of the country...."—*New York Graphic.*

AMSTERDAM.

From "On the Wing Through Europe."

A MOROCCAN WELL.

"'Solitarius' is a series of thoughtful, quaintly written essays.... These drama-novels are readable and pleasing productions by an author who revels in the eccentric..... The volumes are choice in design, and are the very flower of the printer's art."—*New Orleans Picayune.*

"These productions are thoroughly unique."—*Chicago Inter-Ocean.*

"The drama-novels are awake and alive; and that is no small virtue when so many published books are torpid... 'The Venetian Study' is logical and impressive. The works of this author must be regarded as very promising."—*Boston Herald.*

"The drama-novels are capital stories, well told, and equally brilliant."—*Evening Telegram.*

"Barns is both a philosopher and a poet. His prose is stately, strong, and graceful; his poems are exalted in tone, majestic in style.... The drama-novels are the productions of a master of English, an artist in description, and display a rare versatility.... This young author's work is introduced to the public in a most attractive form.... The series is of great value."—*Minneapolis Journal.*

"Barns is thoroughly in earnest, and is filled with the consciousness of the solemnity of his mission, and of the urgent need there is in the world for the truth his art would teach.... The poems show a true, workmanlike touch, and 'Solitarius' is a work of truth and brilliancy."—*Chicago Tribune.*

"The author of these books has read much, travelled widely, and thought deeply, and is enabled to use these conditions with effect in his writings which are elevated in tone, in philosophy breathing a hopeful, independent spirit, while the reader is not allowed to forget that he is an American... The poems are distinguished by an elevation of sentiment, and a definite purpose."—*Albany Journal.*

" Barns is a thoughtful man and a skilful workman. The French, it is plain, have not a monopoly of epigrams. His works are worth reading for their thoughtfulness and their suggestiveness, a line often standing for a whole page, and occult thoughts are put in so rational a way as to disarm criticism aud charm acceptance. As to eccentricities—well, who would live forever in a dull, flat country."—*Christian Union.*

"The versatility of this author is shown by the simultaneous issue of three volumes entirely distinct in scope and style. .... The novels show dramatic power and a weirdness of imagination... The poems are reflective and philosophic often, and show a poetic fancy combined with depth of feeling. In ' Solitarius' there are scattered gems of thought, suggestive and inspiring."—*Brooklyn Times.*

" What a drama-novel is can only be imagined by one who has had the pleasure of reading Mr. Barns. . . . They are written in a light and amusing style. They are welcome."—*Nassau Lit. Review, Princeton College.*

" Ambitious in its serious thoughtfulness. His evident honesty and high purpose makes us wish him all they merit."—*Critic.*

" Well worthy all the refinements of the book-maker's art which they bear. Satire and wisdom alternate with commonplace phrases ; but there is real thought beneath the words, and many of the strangest sentences are full of suggestion. Mr. Barns has had exceptional advatanges and wide experience of many kinds of life, and he has evidently thought much before he has written at all."—*Writer.*

" New York's Rising Litterateur."—Article in *Chicago Herald.*

" These several works bear an individuality not to be mistaken. Of Mr. Barns' critics the hypercritical admit that here is an author who gives extraordinary promise of the future."—*The Author*, Boston.

From "AS 'TIS IN LIFE."

From "IN WESTERN LEVANT."

www.ingramcontent.com/pod-product-compliance
Lightning Source LLC
Chambersburg PA
CBHW021829230426
43669CB00008B/907